ARZAK

Secrets

Published in 2015 by
Grub Street
4 Rainham Close
London
SW11 6SS

Email: food@grubstreet.co.uk
Web: www.grubstreet.co.uk
Twitter: @grub_street
Facebook: Grub Street Publishing

Reprinted 2015, 2016

First published in Spanish by Bainet editorial S.A.
Text copyright © Juan Mari Arzak
Copyright this English language edition © Grub Street 2015
Translated by Heather Maisner

A CIP catalogue record for this book is available from the British Library.

ISBN 978-1-910690-08-6

Printed and bound in Slovenia

AZAK

Secrets

GRUB STREET • LONDON

Prologue

It isn't particularly difficult to explain the intention of this book to curious readers. The title is highly significant. The idea of culinary secrets takes us back in time to an outdated belief in jealously guarding recipes and culinary formulae, as if they were 'cloths of gold'. This secrecy was so great that in many restaurants, individuals, mainly apprentices, were forced to give back or hide any sauce or dish, invented by the chef of the house, that they had finished off or flavoured in a personal way. One story reveals this perfectly. Everyone knows about Russian salad, a dish that has long been popular in many places, not only here but throughout Europe. This salad was known as 'Salad Olivier', as it still is in classical recipes. It seems that in 1860 the French chef Lucien Olivier, who was co-owner of the Hermitage, a trendy restaurant in Moscow's Trubnaya Square, created a motley salad that was an immediate success. But following the guidelines of the time, the chef kept secret, not only the ingredients in his recipe, but also all the spices and seasonings. What's more, he went to the grave (I believe he is certainly buried in the Moscow cemetery) with the secrets of that salad. Only after questioning many Hermitage diners, who had enjoyed the dish at the time, could the Olivier salad ingredients and different dressings be unravelled in a more or less verbal way. Today this is unthinkable. At any event, the secrets of our cookery can be said to be 'open secrets', constantly disseminated through works like this, newspapers and magazines of all kinds, as well as countless websites and internet blogs, providing information to the entire planet in seconds. Far from being a handkerchief, the world is now a tablecloth.

Therefore, 'the secrets' mentioned in this book are nothing but the wide open doors of our kitchen. Particularly our research laboratory, discovering many, many small cookery products and new techniques, ideas for fun combinations, visual explosions that help with the understanding of the cuisine's recipes, which, without denying the complexity, sometimes opt for simple, but not simplistic, solutions, in that what really matters is the very occurrence of their creation. All this is based on the apt words of the great artist Javier Mariscal, 'when in doubt, simplicity'.

Furthermore, I do not have sleepless nights trying to summarize the secret of the newness of Arzak's cuisine, as you can infer from reading this book.

It is a cuisine with a very specific personality, responding to the taste and expertise of those who make up the team that researches and produces this cuisine. But of course, we are not Martians, and it is a Basque cuisine with concrete roots and above all tastes, that can be called idiosyncratic tastes (ways of being, in this case, eating, collective ownership, Basque), to be respected and not thrown overboard. Another key facet of our culinary work is that of research, an important factor in the development of all enterprises and, of course, the most creative. I like to emphasize that Arzak is no longer a lone person, who, in his day, why not say it, was a precursor, travelled, courageous, always with great boldness. It is a team, who investigates, tastes and tests everything and gives the best, i.e., shows diners eager for new experiences, only a small percentage, the minimum best of that which has been investigated. Precisely because this is an evolutionary cuisine, not a culinary success dying or living off the greatness of a series of perfect formulas in technique or taste. And it needs to be constantly moving forward in order not to stagnate. And that brings us to the end of these definitions: it is an avant-garde cuisine, which is not cloning other leading cuisines or has few that are similar, surrenders to no-one, but prefers to lead, with all the risks involved, and, along with other great chefs, to keep Basque cuisine and therefore also Spanish cuisine, at the spearhead of permanent renovation in the world.

I believe this work is a small sample of the above. Especially in the aspect I wish to highlight. Teamwork. Thus, in the creation and practical development of these recipes, as always, the entire team has bent over backwards. From my daughter Elena, who contributed many ideas, thoughts and suggestions; to chef, Pello Aramburu (and everyone around him), above all with their practical qualifications, and, of course, at the heart of responsibility, Xabi Gutiérrez, creative head of our research laboratory, and another key person, his right hand man, the young Igor Zalakain, who painstakingly synthesized all creations into practice. We cannot forget the importance of the visual element today and, through the front door, here comes the hugely professional photographer and close friend, Mikel Alonso, who unusually in the graphic collaboration of many less impressive books, takes us stunningly through the eye to the essence of each recipe. Nor can I fail to include in our team, the pen of another great friend and collaborator Mikel Corcuera, who can interpret what I think better than anyone, and with whom once again, I have easily been able to provide the glossary to our unique cookbook with precision and depth.

I also have to thank my good friends the Spanish publishers Bainet Editorial, who again bet on us to produce a complex work that will hopefully enjoy success to be shared for the good of all. And to Grub Street, the publishers of the English edition.

Juan Mari

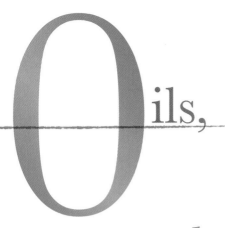ils,
new colours,
aromas and flavours

About twenty years ago, I started to experiment with smoothies or vegetable, herb and fruit juices, incorporating them into different types of oils. From the start, and also in later research, the cookery team and I prepared and tested many combinations.

It is undoubtedly common in cookery, above all in the Mediterranean (especially in the most modern cookery – and the author's), to use these oils in profusion. Aromatic oils increase the taste quality of a dish. They are easy to prepare, in terms of combinations of ingredients, because there are hundreds of them... just unleash the imagination of each cook. Basil or parsley, tarragon or rosemary, with spinach or garlic, with lemon, orange or tangerine peel, passion fruit and other exotic fruits, with oils sweet or spicy. Also with cardamom, green pepper or cinnamon. I recall some dishes that gave almost more attention to these details, and the taste of the

aromatic oils in sauces and, especially, in vinaigrettes, that enhanced the raw material of the dish. Base oils: of course, our fantastic extra virgin olive oil but also walnut, peanut, corn, hazelnut or sunflower oil.

Prawns en escabeche, marinated with a striking and equally tasty beetroot oil. Baby squid grilled in corn oil with a sweet corn smoothie, or a squid oil to enhance a mackerel with chive vinaigrette. A unique olive oil with chorizo for cod with 'kokotxas' Pil Pil. And for a light dessert, a neutral sunflower oil flavoured with vanilla, escorting a pineapple cooked in rum with hazelnut foam. And so on, to name a few dishes I find hard to forget.

One of our latest offerings is a creamy avocado oil, a subtle touch in a broth of tomato, peach and vinegar, marinating slices of bonito covered with cheese foam.

tomato with cheese

ingredients

6 people

For the stock

80 g peach flesh
1 tablespoon sugar
250 g ripe tomatoes
20 g extra virgin olive oil
70 g avocado oil
1 tablespoon sherry vinegar
salt
black pepper

For cubes of marinated bonito

100 g bonito
250 ml water
250 ml white wine vinegar
50 ml olive oil
salt

For cheese foam

300 g milk
100 g smoked Idiazabal cheese, with rind
100 g cream

and a touch of avocado

method

For the stock

Cut the peach flesh and sauté lightly with sugar. Chop the tomatoes and mash them together with the peach; emulsify with olive and avocado oils. Strain through a chinois, add the vinegar and season.

For the cubes of marinated bonito

Cut tuna in chunks and marinate in the mixture of water and vinegar for half an hour. Drain and place in the olive oil until used.

For the cheese foam

Blend all the ingredients and strain through a chinois. Fill the siphon, tighten the cap and shake. Remove the cap and leave to stand in the refrigerator. Pour the contents of the siphon over liquid nitrogen. Leave it to harden well and then break it up.

Drain the marinated tuna cubes, add a pinch of salt, place in a bowl and pour the tomato and peach broth over them. Place the cold cheese foam over the broth.

Sea vegetables

Many years ago, in the introduction to his landmark book *The Kitchen Market*, my great friend Paul Bocuse used a prescient sentence that really got me thinking: 'These days, whoever wants to get on, must go round the world. And', he continued: 'Whenever I move to a new country, I return brimming with ideas.' Our new food movement of the seventies captured this need and introduced – if only in an incipient way – the use of exotic algae, together with other products which are now almost common place.

In the Western world, sea vegetables have mostly been hailed for their medicinal properties to the detriment of their great culinary possibilities: even the ancient Greeks and Romans ignored them. Only along the coasts of Britain and the British Isles, has there been a tradition – for some thousand years – of consuming the algae that proliferate along these coasts, for example sea lettuce, which is sometimes added to oatmeal cakes.

By contrast, for over ten thousand years seaweeds have been an essential element in the diet of most Asian populations, particularly the Japanese, where there are extraordinary dishes that use different types of algae.

It is important to note that there are many kinds of algae and, not only does each have a different flavour and texture, but also a different culinary use. Thus, kombu, known as *Laminaria gigante*, is the basis of the delicious Japanese stocks, the dashi. Furthermore, when added to vegetables, it softens them and makes them more digestible. One of the best-known algae is perhaps nori, sold in sheets, and recognisable as a wrapper on the equally famous sushi.

And how can one not mention agar agar (*Gelidium cantilagineum*), a gelatineous red algae, very flexible and resilient despite its intricate branches. It is also known by the following names: agar, gelosina, vegetable gelatine, Chinese gelatine, and Japanese fish tail.

Its extract, also called agar agar, is colourless and tasteless, and absorbs water between 200 and 300 times its weight, forming a gelatine.

Culinarily it is important because it is a gel that maintains its gelling power when both warm and hot, which does not happen with other gelatines that only do so when cold.

Lamb with Café 'Cortado'

ingredients

4 people

For the raisin sauce

40 g raisins
15 g brandy
35 g fried almonds
1 small tomato
20 g cooked garlic
15 g virgin olive oil
1 tablespoon sherry vinegar
salt
pepper

For the lamb

800 g rack of lamb (200 g per serving)

For the lamb sauce

500 g lamb bones
2 onions
1 clove garlic
250 ml water
250 ml lamb stock
1 small onion
safflower threads
salt
pepper

For the mint leaves

12 mint leaves
50 ml olive oil

For the veils of milk coffee

2 g decaffinated coffee powder
8 g agar agar
1.5 g icing sugar
1.5 g powdered milk

In addition

virgin olive oil
safflower threads

For the raisin sauce

Blend all ingredients and season. Set aside.

For the lamb

Thoroughly clean the rack and cut into portions.
Coat the pieces with the sauce and brown well on both sides.
Set aside.

For the lamb sauce

Colour the bones slightly with a dash of oil. Add garlic and
onions cut into strips and sauté for a few minutes.
Deglaze and moisten with the lamb stock and the water.
Cook on a low flame for 2 hours. Strain. Add the onion cut into
thin rings and the safflower threads. Season with salt and pepper.

For the mint leaves

Blanch in boiling water. Then cool well, spread out and crush.
Cover with the oil and set aside.

For the veils of milk coffee

Mix all ingredients and reduce them to powder.
Grease a 10 x 20 cm plastic mould with a little oil.
Distribute the powder and shake the mould so that the excess
falls off. Cook the mould upside down in a steamer at 119°C
for 15 seconds.Remove from the steamer and remove the veil
that will have formed in the mould.

Spread the mint over the bottom of a dish along
with a few strands of safflower and a few drops of oil.
Arrange the lamb in the centre of the dish, wrapped
in the veil, giving height and volume to the whole.
In this way present it to the diners, with the sauce in a
separate jug. In front of the diners, pour the very hot
sauce over the veil, making it disappear.

Lamb with green sponge cake

ingredients

4 people

For the green sauce

50 g olive oil, 25 g spinach purée, 10 g pistachio paste,
25 g codium algae, the pulp of a passion fruit, 15 g green papaya, ½ kiwi (peeled),
25 g fried almonds, salt, pepper

For the lamb

800 g rack of lamb (200 g per serving)

For the pistachio sponge cake

3 eggs, 60 g sugar, 60 g flour, 15 g spinach purée, 2.5 g freeze-dried spinach,
10 g nori seaweed, 2.5 g green tea

For the green oil

60 g olive oil, 60 g parsley (stems included), 5 g nori seaweed, salt

For the lamb sauce

500 g lamb bones, 1 clove garlic, 2 onions, 1 shallot, 250 ml water,
250 ml lamb stock, salt, pepper, safflower threads

For the melting sheet

100 g cocoa butter, 3 g freeze-dried parsley, 3 g freeze-dried barley,
3 g freeze-dried chives, 1 g salt

In addition

green papaya, cut in cubes
mint, cut into small pieces
parsley powder
fried papaya seeds

method

Place the squares of papaya, fried papaya seeds, chopped mint, crumbled pistachio sponge cake and parsley powder on the bottom of a dish. Arrange the lamb in the centre of the dish and lightly season.
At the table and in front of the diners, place the melting sheets over the lamb, making them disappear, contributing the oily touch to the dish.

For the green sauce

Purée all ingredients, forming a paste. Season and reserve.

For the lamb

Thoroughly clean the rack and cut into portions.
Coat the pieces with the sauce and brown well on both sides. Set aside.

For the pistachio sponge cake

Beat the eggs with the sugar until they are thick and foamy. Gently add the flour without letting the mixture collapse. At the last moment, gently incorporate the spinach mixture, shredded nori and tea. Bake in a cake mould at 180°C for 18 minutes. Remove from mould and set aside.

For the green oil

Purée the ingredients. Strain and season lightly. Set aside.

For the lamb sauce

Colour the bones lightly with a dash of oil. Add the garlic, onions and shallot cut into strips and sauté for a few minutes. Deglaze and moisten with the stock and the water.
Cook over a low heat for 90 minutes. Strain and add a pinch of salt and pepper. Finish the sauce by adding 60 g of green oil and a pinch of safflower.

For the melting sheet

Melt the butter at under 60°C. Add the remaining ingredients.
Spread in a thin layer over two sheets of greaseproof paper. Leave to cool. Once cold, cut it and store in the refrigerator.

Crayfish on mushroom and seaweed 'lichen'

ingredients

4 people

For the crayfish

8 crayfish (at least 100 g each)
100 ml olive oil
20 g mushroom powder
salt
ginger
liquorice powder

For the corn sauce

50 ml olive oil
1 onion
the crayfish heads
1 vanilla pod
100 g fresh corn
salt
pepper

For the black mushroom sauce

1 onion
100 g corn mushroom powder (huitlacoche)
10 g Marcona almonds
50 ml olive oil
salt
ground ginger

For the crispy mushroom

350 g corn water
100 g corn oil
40 g cornflour (corn starch)
10 g corn mushroom powder (huitlacoche)

For the vinaigrette

100 ml olive oil
5 g beer yeast
10 g brie cheese rind
10 g rice vinegar
5 g sugar
1 g lavender
salt
pepper

For the fried seaweed

200 g sea lettuce (*Ulva rigida*)
1 clove garlic, chopped
2 tablespoons olive oil

In addition

50 g fresh ground
   corn (add a little water if necessary)
virgin olive oil

method

For the crayfish

Split the crayfish in half and place the body to one side and the pinchers and head to the other. Keep the heads for the sauce and save the pinchers for other uses.
Place a skewer lengthwise through each crayfish so that the tails do not bend during cooking. Blanch lightly in boiling water and then cool rapidly in iced water. Peel them. Season with salt and pepper and lightly season with ginger and liquorice powder. At the last moment, cook over a high heat and add the mushroom and oil mixture. Set aside.

For the corn sauce

Clean the onion, cut and fry it in a pan with half the oil. Then add the crayfish heads and sauté together. Add the corn and the vanilla pod cut in half. Cover with water and cook for 1 hour. Remove the vanilla and blend. Strain through a chinois and season.

For the black mushroom sauce

Clean the onion, cut and fry it in a pan with half the oil. Add the remaining ingredients. Lightly cook then grind to a paste. Season and add a pinch of ginger.

For the crispy mushroom

Cold mix all the ingredients, except the corn mushroom, and place over the surface of a slightly warm non-stick pan. Allow to evaporate completely so that it becomes a kind of a crispy lichen. Remove and sprinkle with powdered corn mushroom. Store in a dry place until used.

For the vinaigrette

Slightly chop the cheese rind and cold mix it with the rest of the ingredients. Add salt and pepper.

For the fried seaweed

De-salt the seaweed in cold water for approximately 2 hours. Drain well and sauté with the chopped garlic.

Add the fresh corn purée to 50 g of the corn sauce. Bring to the boil and add a tablespoon of virgin olive oil.

Spread the corn sauce across both sides of the dish. Heat the dish on the salamander so that the sauce dries quickly. Arrange the crayfish, seasoned with the vinaigrette, in the centre of the dish and place the crunchy 'lichen' over the crayfish.

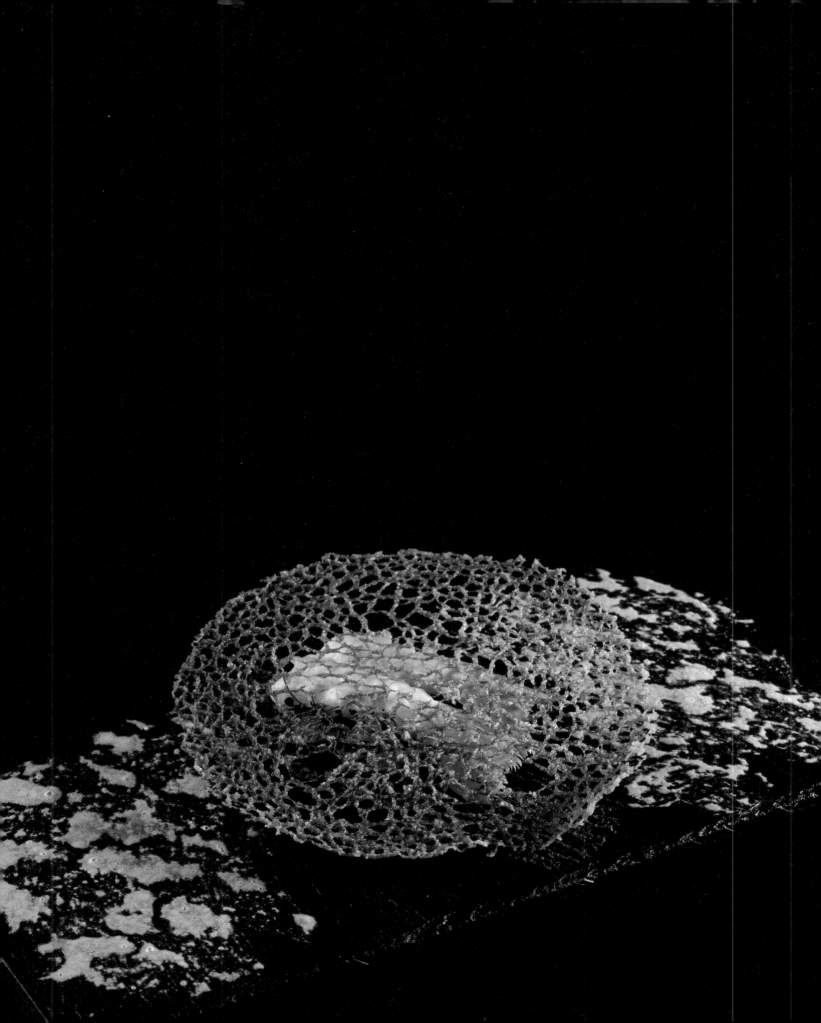

The flavour

Is there anyone who doesn't know, or hasn't heard about, clay, also known as kaolin or kaolinite, a very pure white clay, which is used to make porcelain and primers for starching. It is also used in some medications and for producing cosmetics, and when the quality isn't very pure, it's used to manufacture paper.

The word kaolin comes from the Chinese kao = high and ling = hill, indicating the place in Jiangxi Province, near Jauchu Fa, where the Chinese first encountered this type of natural clay. Since ancient times it has also been used as a healing agent in many cultures. Like other clays, such as green clay, it is rich in hydrated aluminium silicates but poor in trace elements. It also contains significant amounts of other minerals, such as magnesium, calcium, copper, zinc, cobalt, iron and selenium.

It has antibacterial, anti-inflammatory and healing qualities. And for internal use, it protects the gastric and intestinal mucus as it speeds up healing. It helps capture harmful substances, adheres to them and then drags them to the outside. For external use, it can be applied as a plaster or mask; it is also interesting as a mouthwash and a powder similar to talcum powder for babies.

What is new is the sudden use of this natural product in cookery, as introduced by the most creative and cutting-edge chefs: among others, Andoni Luis Adúriz, chef at Mugaritz of Errenteria, with his great 'devilry' of 'Potatoes Cooked in Clay' (in this case grey clay) served with a light garlic mayonnaise.

In our case, we use white clay in a creation that has had a great impact, not only visual and for its gustatory delicacy but also because of the uniqueness of the product itself. A dish in which one of the emblematic fish of Basque cuisine, the hake, is combined with the novel clay, which makes a double appearance, both in the sauce under the hake and the curd that escorts it, as well as in the sauce that is initially spread over the fish.

# of porcelain

Hake and white clay

ingredients

4 people

For the white clay sauce

20 g toasted bread
30 g toasted pine nuts
100 g olive oil
5 g white clay
30 g gently sautéed leek
salt
ground pepper
chopped parsley

For the hake

4 hake fillets (150 g per serving)
freeze-dried hake powder

For the white clay paint

25 g Marcona almonds
25 g pine nuts
50 ml olive oil
15 g sugar
10 g coconut flesh
3 tablespoons white Martini
500 g fish fumet
10 g white clay
salt
pepper

For the green sauce and veal cheek juice

150 g salsa verde
20 g stewed veal cheek sauce
15 g olive oil
salt
pepper

For the clay curd

¼ head of garlic
¼ Zopako bread (not overly toasted)
500 g water
60 g onion
50 g leek
25 g fresh garlic
10 g Marcona almonds
15 g pine nuts
5 g sugar
10 g coconut flesh
2 tablespoons white Martini
250 g fish fumet
10 g white clay
agar agar (1g for each 100g)
olive oil
salt
pepper

To discolour the parsley

50 g parsley leaves
250 ml ethyl alcohol

method

For the white clay sauce

Blend all of the ingredients to form a paste. Season with salt and pepper and add the chopped parsley.

For the hake

To make the freeze-dried powder (a pinch), rapidly sauté 100 g of hake meat with a drop of oil and insert into the freeze drier; it will take about 40 hours to dehydrate. Once dry, grind to powder. Add the freeze-dried hake powder to the hake, coat with the white clay sauce and cook a la plancha. Set aside.

For the white clay paint

Lightly fry the almonds and pine nuts in a pan with oil until golden. Then add the sugar, coconut and the Martini. Sauté and moisten with the fish fumet. Reduce to half and add the clay. Blend together and season with salt and pepper.

For the green sauce and veal cheek salsa

Mix the green sauce with the stewed veal cheek sauce. Bring to a light boil and cut the sauce with the olive oil. Add salt and pepper.

For the clay curd

Peel the garlic and brown in oil. Add the Zopako bread, sliced and toasted. Cover with water and cook 45 minutes. Set aside.
Clean the vegetables, cut finely and gently sauté with a little oil, but do not allow to colour. Set aside. Lightly brown the almonds and pine nuts in a pan with oil. Then add the sugar, coconut, and the Martini. Soften until slightly reduced and moisten with the fumet. Bring to a boil and add the clay. Blend together. Boil all the ingredients and add the agar agar (1 g for each 100 g). Add a pinch of salt and pepper. Once cool, cut the dough into cubes.

For the discoloured parsley

Leave the parsley leaves covered in alcohol for three hours until the spirit evaporates. The leaves will be pale, discoloured and crispy.

Draw a perfect square with the white clay paint on a dinner plate and place the hake on it. To its side place the clay curd and sink the discoloured parsley leaves into it. Drizzle the hake with the green sauce and veal cheek juice.

Clay bonbon

ingredients

4 people

For the truffle

250 g chocolate 70% cocoa
100 g cream 35% fat
50 g whole milk
1 g tandoori masala powder

For the Rooibos infusion

2 g Rooibos (*Aspalathus linearis*)
130 g water

For the clay

100 g Rooibos tea infusion
30 g white clay
4 g chopped parsley

method

For the truffle

Chop the chocolate. Set aside.
Boil the milk with the cream for 30 seconds.
Pour the mixture over the chocolate, little
by little, until you get an homogeneous
mixture. Add the tandoori powder. Leave
to cool in small semi spherical moulds for
at least 6 hours. Join the spherical halves,
applying heat, to achieve perfect spheres.
Allow to cool. Thread onto separate
skewers and set aside.

For the rooibos infusion

Boil the water and add the Rooibos off the
heat. Leave to infuse for three minutes and
strain. Leave to cool and reserve.

For the clay

Cold mix the ingredients to make a thick
dough.

Dip the spheres into the clay,
covering them with a thin layer.
Dry with cold air until the clay
hardens. Store in the refrigerator.
They are served on a marble base.

Always in fashion

Llibre de el Sent Soví – a 14th century work written in Catalan by an anonymous cook to the King of England – mentions rice (*Oryza sativa*) as an ingredient in Menjar blanc (Blancmange). An emulsion of almonds with rice, a kind of porridge, to which were added the broth and meat of chickens or capons, relating it to the Navarre Christmas canas (white hair) soup. It isn't until the 15th century, in Nola Ruperto's *El libre del Coch* where two formulas for stewed rice appear, that can be considered antecedents to the multiple stewed rice dishes that would arise in later centuries – especially for the Eastern Spanish – who naturally included them in their cuisine. They were rice with beef broth and rice baked in the oven. The latter is made in the oven with egg yolks and a crust, very similar to its 'great-grandson', *arros rossejat*, toasted rice, or rice with a crust, so popular today in Valencia . . .

Today, it is not only the quality of rice that is important, we also pay attention to the area of the produce or to the characteristics of the grain (long, short, brown, etc) for, as is the case with the fashion for varietal wines, little by little, deep reflection is being imposed on the varieties of rice suitable for each type of preparation. Thus, the same rice is not used for a paella or a dry baked dish as it is for a soupy rice in a pot. Or a risotto or a cooked rice garnish, for which we would choose long-grain American rice, called Thaibonnet in Europe. Not to mention an oriental type of dish, in which case we always go for an aromatic basmati, or a rice with Thai jasmine perfume, or even a sticky or glutinous Japanese rice. The crux of the matter lies in choosing the most suitable variety

for each dish. The Italians, who know a bit about this, specify the type of rice used in all their recipes. With some, especially large stock preparations, they use the variety called arborio, of larger grain, while most of the great Italian creamy rice dishes are prepared with carnaroli, the most elegant and also more expensive Italian rice, or with the smaller but very effective vialone nano.

In our case we have used rice to create something as much in vogue as the crunch in a snack, combined with black beans (which look like coffee beans), traditionally called Moors and Christians in Central America and the Caribbean, but in a very modern, and acclaimed, version.

Rice crackers and 'coffee'

ingredients

For the rice purée

200 g rice
600 g water

For the crackers

400 g cooked and mashed black beans
200 g broth from the beans
700 g rice purée
salt
pepper

For the coffee powder

100 g icing sugar
4 g freeze-dried coffee

In addition

cooked whole beans
bacon slices
oil for frying

method

For the rice purée

Cook over a low heat for 30 minutes. Mash it all but do not strain it.

For the crackers

Cook the black beans in abundant salted water; separate, on the one hand, the beans and, on the other hand, their cooking broth. Weigh the beans and the broth and blend thoroughly with the rice puree.
Roll out the dough on greaseproof paper and cut into rounds about 7 cm in diameter. Place some strips of bacon on the top of each of them with a few cooked beans, which will be like coffee beans. Leave to dry for 24 hours at 50°C.

For the coffee powder

Cold mix the ingredients. Set aside.

Fry the crackers in abundant oil, place them on trays and sprinkle with the coffee powder.

A very versatile giant

The baobab (*Adansonia digitata*) is an enormous tree that is very useful to the African people. It can be said to be as beneficial there, as much if not more, than pork or duck are to us. In the nutritional sense, it produces a fruit called monkey bread, the size of a small melon, which contains large amounts of vitamin C. This fruit is rich in fibre and is an excellent human food, consumed as a paste and made into a natural drink. Fibre from baobab bark is used to manufacture ropes and baskets, and even the wet pollen is used as glue. And what interested us most in a culinary way, is that in many African countries they make excellent soups with the boiled leaves.

There are species such as the African baobab that, without reaching great heights, have widths that would be the envy of the great redwoods. The *Adansonia digitata* is a species native to the semi-arid regions of sub-Saharan Africa, although it has been introduced to many tropical countries. It usually reaches 20 metres in height but its trunk can be more than 10 metres in diameter. The baobab is like a huge barrel that stores up to 120,000 litres of water. The hollowed trunks of the baobab have had many picturesque uses. They have served as a prison, house, barn, stable... It's said that a baobab in Zimbabwe, made into a bus stop, can hold up to 40 people. Baobab trees can live 3,000 years or more.

Its strange appearance has earned it a place in numerous African legends: it is said that a person, who drinks water with baobab seeds in it, will be protected from attack by crocodiles; and, if someone dares to pull out a baobab flower, they will die, eaten by a lion.

It is curious that elephants find them irresistible, not only eating young green plants but also digesting the smooth wood of the trunk, weakening the tree with tusks and trunks to the extent that sometimes the tree dies or falls; it is common to find dead trees in areas where elephants eat or in the vicinity of the lakes where they come to drink.

We have used its delicate tasting leaves together with olive oil as a sauce, enhancing the flavour of a very summery fish like northern bonito, without overwhelming its properties. Also its powdered leaves, together with powdered tuna, are very powerful, and used to balance the sauce for the recipe.

bonito baobab

ingredients

4 people

For the bonito fillets

600 g bonito (140 g per serving)
salt
ginger

For the bonito brine

75 g salt
1 litre lemon verbena infusion
(25 g lemon verbena per litre of water)

For the baobab sauce

100 g olive oil
20 g powdered baobab leaves

For the baobab salsa

2 onions sautéed
1 litre water
5 g powdered tuna
3 g powdered baobab leaves
salt
ginger

For the bonito bridge

150 g isomalt
15 g powdered tuna

For the melon radish

4 radishes
50 g melon
3 chopped lemon verbena leaves
2 tablespoons olive oil
salt
pepper

In addition

fennel leaves
pansy petals

method

For the bonito fillets

Cut the tuna in rectangles, calculating 2 per serving.

For the bonito brine

Thoroughly cold-mix the salt into the infusion. Add the bonito fillets and leave for 10 minutes.

For the baobab sauce

Mix both ingredients well and spread over the bonito fillets before cooking a la plancha.

For the baobab salsa

Mix all ingredients in a saucepan and cook for 5 minutes. Blend and strain. Season and add a pinch of ginger.

For the bonito bridge

Melt the isomalt over medium heat in a saucepan. When the temperature reaches 180°C, add the powdered tuna. Spread the caramel thinly between two sheets of paper. Before it is completely cold, cut into rectangles and store in a dry place.

For the melon radishes

Thoroughly clean the radishes and core them (as if they were apples) with the help of a small tube.
Cut the melon into small cylinders, which we will later place in the radishes. Sauté lightly with a drop of oil. Sprinkle with lemon verbena and season.
Fill the radishes with the melon and cook in the pan with a little oil over a low heat. Season.

Grill the bonito fillets, leaving them very juicy.
Spread a little of the salsa and a few fennel
leaves on a plate and place the fillets on them.
Place the radish to one side and make a bridge
between both with the sheet of isomalt and tuna.
Sprinkle leaves over the bridge.

So ancient,

At the outset it should be noted that a sprout is any seed whose metabolism is activated when it comes into contact with heat, water and air.

It has quite rightly been said that the use of germinated seeds or sprouts in food and medicine is twice as old as the great wall of China. And that both the Chinese and the Japanese germinated soybeans, mung and barley, as animal supplements. On the other hand, in the West, a description of simple germination techniques is found in the writings of the Essenes, who lived in Israel and Egypt at the time of Christ, and, later, both Vasco da Gama and Magellan were able to make their long journeys thanks to the sprouts that protected their crew from scurvy. Similarly, Captain Cook could travel for more than three years without any member of his crew dying from scurvy due to lack of vitamin C, by daily providing them with tea made from sprouting beans. Sprouts have the enormous advantage that their seeds can be stored for years, are transported easily, are digested and assimilated very easily by the body and are really cheap and, in addition, they are foods of great biological quality.

Sprouts are one of the few foods that we eat while they are still alive, and this simple fact exponentially increases their nutritional value, which remains intact until the moment we eat them. They then help with their own digestion, allowing the body to rest and be regenerated. On the other hand,

So modern

their wealth of live enzymes, chlorophyll, amino acids, minerals, vitamins and trace elements makes them whole foods that can help to correct the shortcomings of modern food. Sprouts are a concentrate of substances generating health, natural substances, that life itself develops in a much more perfect form than any complex laboratory. They are also the least contaminated foods that we can find, because for a grain to germinate, it has to be of a good enough quality to do so, as with a certain level of pollution, plants cease to be able to reproduce.

Finally, some foods, perhaps not widely known, are beginning to be used extensively, not only in restaurants but also for home cooking, as you can cultivate them and keep them at home quite easily. The most important thing is that the seeds come from plants that have been grown organically, without toxic chemicals, and thus retain their germinating power.

A wide range of seeds can be used for germination. To cite but some, alfalfa, so rich and full, refreshing green soybeans, wheat, so sweet and healthy, powerful fenugreek (typical in the Middle East), the Asian adzuki beans and lentils, very delicate. As well as chickpeas, sunflower, onion, garlic, endive, fennel, rice, radishes, mustard, or even some as curious as quinoa, clover or poppy.

Harry Potter's cauldron

I recall something funny that happened to me at the restaurant regarding the fashionable topic of using dry ice or CO2 or, as it is also more elegantly called, carbonic snow. It was one of the first times we used this product in front of a customer. In a dessert called 'Strawberry Bubbles', a strawberry milkshake is poured onto a container holding the aforementioned dry ice and, instantly, bubbles – which seem to overflow without end and comes spurting up, resulting in a great spectacle. A few really surprised diners told me that all I needed was 'a pointed hat'. Of course, they were referring to Harry Potter and his bubbling cauldron. Without doubt, the right impact had been achieved.

Elaborating on the theme, aside from this amusing anecdote, we must clarify some points about this new product, increasingly better known as dry ice rather than CO2 in solid state, because it goes directly from a solid state to a gaseous state, without passing through the liquid state (hence the word dry). The process is known – by the beautiful word – sublimation. It is called ice, not only because it is in a solid state, but also because it is cold, and so icy that it burns, at nothing less than minus 78 °C.

But this has long been in use in laboratories and hospitals, and it has an even more usual and everyday use in pubs and breweries, in particular, for cooling beer served from the tap or barrel.

In this case, the CO2 in liquid form has to be at very high pressure, and when coming out of the canister, therefore, supports a very strong decompression and passes into gaseous form; this causes a rapid cooling of the liquid, part of which does not evaporate completely into a solid CO2 state (for this you need to reach the temperature of about 8 °C) To catch it, what is employed, in hospitality parlance, is called a pillbox (in the best sense of the word), which is simply a container where the dry ice that will be formed is collected and looks like a tablet.

Therefore, the explanation of the aforementioned bubbles is less magical than it appears. By immersing dry ice in liquid, it immediately passes into gas, and begins to bubble (CO2 is released, which is the same gas for soft drinks, beer or champagne). If, for example, we put it at the bottom of a bowl and add milk (in our case a lactic fruit shake) many, many bubbles are quickly released and stay trapped in the foam by milk proteins, which are known to be magnificent foaming agents. These bubbles explode, releasing hazy smoke, which is condensed water vapour. Magic has its tricks.

Pineapple bubbles

ingredients

For the pineapple dressing

60 g sugar
1 g dried thyme
1 g dried Marjoram
1 g liquorice powder
1 g powdered ginger
1 g black pepper powder
1 g dry parsley powder

For the roasted pineapple

½ pineapple
2 vanilla pods
9 nails
40 g brown sugar

For the piña colada

½ can coco López (210 g)
500 ml pineapple juice
45 g milk
140 g cream
60 g aged rum

In addition

1 glass tube 6 cm high
25 g crushed dry ice

method

For the pineapple dressing

Mix all the ingredients. Set aside.

For the grilled pineapple

Peel and core the pineapple and cut into three pieces.
Cut the vanilla pods in half. Go through each piece of pineapple with a half vanilla. Drive in the nails and cover with sugar. Roast under the grill at medium heat. When done, remove the nails and vanilla. Reserve a piece of pineapple and roast it in the oven for another 10 minutes at 190°C, mash and strain it. Reserve the juice.
Cut the rest of the pineapple into portions. Set aside.

For the piña colada

Mix all the ingredients to form an homogeneous mixture. Keep cold until used.

Place the pineapple in a soup bowl with its juice. Place beside it the highball glass with dry ice. Pour the piña colada into the glass and this will exhale bubbles of piña colada. After 45 seconds, remove the glass and the pineapple will appear surrounded by bubbles.

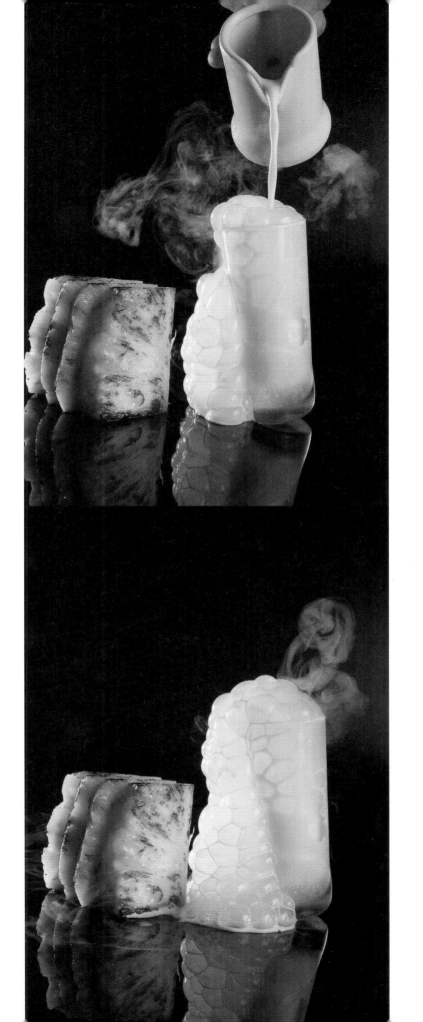

'Boiling cold'

ingredients

100 g vodka
150 g sugar
200 g tonic
100 g water
zest of 2 lemons
pinch of nutmeg
pinch of ground pepper
4 chopped basil leaves
4 chopped mint leaves

In addition

20 g dry ice (CO2)

method

First, thoroughly mix the sugar with the vodka. Then add the rest of ingredients.

Place 3 soup spoons of dry ice in a glass cafetière, pour in the prepared liquid and press the lid down to cause – through this pressure and the reaction of the dry ice – the 'boiling cold'.

bubbling carrot soup

ingredients

method

4 people

For the bubbling carrot soup

300 g water
70 g sugar
½ vanilla pod
20 g orange liqueur
2.6 g xanthan gum

For the carrot purée

600 g carrots, diced
6 tablespoons olive oil
½ vanilla pod
½ cinnamon stick
30 g coconut milk
Pinch of nutmeg

For the carrot cake

500 g carrot purée
3 egg yolks
1 egg
80 g butter
120 g sugar
40 g orange liqueur
40 g liquid cream
15 g cornflour (corn starch)

For the carrot and pumpkin smoothie

200 g pumpkin juice
100 g carrot juice
50 g sugar
40 g red Vermouth

method

For the bubbling carrot soup

Heat the water in a saucepan with the sugar and the vanilla pod, with its seeds removed. As this comes to the boil, add the orange liqueur and the xanthan gum. Blend together and leave to stand for one hour. Introduce the mixture into a siphon, charging it twice.

For the carrot purée

Poach the carrot in the oil. Add the vanilla pod, without the seeds, and cinnamon. When the carrot is ready, remove the cinnamon and vanilla and add the coconut milk. Add a pinch of nutmeg and blend to a purée.

For the carrot cake

Mix all the ingredients together. Spread the mixture on a silpat and steam bake for 20 minutes.

For the carrot and pumpkin smoothie

Cold mix the ingredients in a blender.

In a sealable jar, first place the carrot cake. Cover it with the carrot and pumpkin smoothie. Spread the foam from the siphon over the surface and immediately close the jar.

A consuming

Since our inception, we have attached particular importance to the use of cocoa and chocolate in the restaurant. And although we mostly use it in desserts, we have also included it in savoury dishes, especially in recent years.

The almost historical prelude to this sweet concert was 'Hot Chocolate Cake with Orange Sauce', which was followed by other leading lights, such as 'Chocolate Spiral', 'Flowing Cocoa Croquettes', 'Cannelloni with Smoked Cocoa', the unique 'Bar of Chocolate, Honey and Tomato', or the no less singular 'Spicy Chocolate Ice Cream' and the anti-globalization, very sarcastically named, 'Chocolate Hamburger', and to these can be added fried chocolate, or the popular ' Ugly Chocolate Tortilla'.

To start with one of the most groundbreaking creations of its day, we can look at smoked cocoa and chocolate. It is well-known that these days we are smoking foods by choice and not obligation. The passage from necessity to pleasure. In line with this thinking about smoking, we realised that we now smoke many products, such as fish, meat, cheese, sausages ... and yet it had not occurred to us to apply this to chocolate, giving it a different dimension after its passage through smoke. The result seemed magical, especially with regard to taste. Something that was also daring and even felt shocking was spicy chocolate. Mexican cuisine gave us the idea to create a spicy chocolate ice cream, which was a great success. The inspiration for this came after we became acquainted with a mole, prepared with lots of cocoa. Although, of course, for European diners we were careful to add hardly any chilli in order not to swamp the overall taste.

It is more traditional to add cocoa and chocolate to savoury dishes in our own culture, as in the legendary recipe 'Partridge with Chocolate'. Perhaps what is more interesting and unique, is to apply this to fish, with prudence and without distorting its virtues or delicacy of taste, as in Hake with 'Incense', in this case cocoa butter.

passion

Soup and chocolate 'among the vines'

ingredients

4 people

For the hot chocolate

200 g dark chocolate, 52% cocoa
1 g powdered liquorice
1 g ginger

For the chocolate clusters

200 g water
6 g methyl

For the chocolate mousse

125 g milk
2.5 g santolina (lavender-cotton)
30 g egg yolk
30 g sugar
2 g gelatine (1 sheet)
1.8 g agar agar
125 g chocolate 52% cocoa
200 g cream, medium whipped

For the strawberries

450 g strawberries
70 g sugar

In addition

fried rolled oats
pansies, cut into thin strips

method

For the hot chocolate

Melt the chocolate in accordance with its characteristics. Mix the remaining ingredients and pour into 48 half-spherical silicone moulds. When hardened, join the chocolate halves together by applying heat to the surfaces to be joined. Set aside.

For the chocolate clusters

Beat both ingredients in a mixer. Leave to rest for 12 hours.
Drill a ball of chocolate with the tip of a thin needle.
Place the chocolate, fastened by the needle, into the mixture of water and methyl. Then leave it stand in water at 80°C for 4 minutes. Repeat this operation with the six spheres of chocolate for each serving.

For the chocolate mousse

In a saucepan, heat the mixture of milk, egg, sugar, santolina, agar agar and gelatine at not more than 75°C. Once heated, pour the mixture over the previously chopped chocolate. Leave to rest until it reaches about 22°C. When this temperature is reached, mix gently to prevent the cream from collapsing. Leave to stand in the fridge.

For the strawberries

Roast the strawberries smothered in sugar at 200°C for 30 minutes. Once roasted, pass through a chinois. Set aside.

Pour 3 soup spoons of prepared strawberries into a hot bowl (55°C). On this, carefully place to one side, the chocolate balls and remove the needle. Place a scoop of mousse beside them and the fried rolled oats on top of the mousse. Sprinkle pansy strips over the dish.

hake
with cocoa incense

ingredients

method

4 people

For the cocoa sauce

35 g cocoa butter, melted
50 g fried almond
½ onion, gently sautéed
30 g peeled pumpkin, sautéed
25 g cooked carrot
50 g sunflower oil
15 g apple cider vinegar
salt
pinch of sugar

For the hake in brine

4 hake fillets (125 g per serving)
500 ml elderflower infusion
30 g fine salt

For mustard leaves

bunch of mustard leaves
olive oil 0.4 °
salt

For the potato and mustard sauces

90 g mustard leaves
20 g parsley leaves
pinch of powdered vinegar
1 normal potato
1 leek
kuzu
salt
pepper

For the sprinkled cocoa

50 g micronized cocoa butter
3 g powdered Espellete peppers
1 g achiote powder
4 g powdered vinegar
pinch of salt

For the cocoa sauce

Blend all ingredients and add melted butter. Season with salt.

For the hake in brine

To prepare the elderflower infusion (500 ml water and 10 g elderflowers), after boiling the water, add the flowers away from the heat. Cover and leave to rest for 5 minutes. Strain.
Dilute the salt in the elderflower infusion, while cold. Immerse the hake fillets in it and leave to rest for 25 minutes. After that time, blot lightly with paper towels. Rub the fish with the sauce and cook it a la plancha. Set aside.

For the mustard leaves

Blanch the mustard leaves in boiling salted water. Cool them quickly so they don't lose their colour and immerse them in oil until used.

For the potato and mustard sauces

For the mustard sauce, cook the mustard and parsley in boiling salted water, then blend and strain. Bind with the kuzu, diluted in water, to make a thick texture.
For the potato sauce, cook the potato with the leek and follow the same procedure as with the mustard sauce.
Salt and pepper both sauces and reserve.

For the sprinkled cocoa

Mix all the ingredients and set aside.

Serve the hake on a shallow dish. Place a few mustard leaves so that they partially cover it. Beside it, place the two sauces, one over the other, without mixing them at all. In front of each diner, sprinkle the cocoa onto the hake so that it melts on contact with the heat.

Its name frightens,

Cod, like pig or duck, can be eaten in its entirety. On the one hand, cod has about five different cuts that make different dishes, when the body is used in the most appropriate way.

But there are also other no less important parts, like the head, which make magnificent spooning dishes. Also the cheeks are highly valued because they are a good substitute for the more expensive hake and possess similar great quantities of gelatine. The tongues, which in the majority of cases are joined to the above, give many a gourmet an exceptional bite. Also the gut, misnamed, as it is really the swimming bladder of the fish, a hydrostatic organ, whose purpose is to change the specific weight/gravity of the animal, enabling it to stay still in the water or ascend and descend at will.

A treatise on food conservation published in Barcelona as long ago as 1832, stated: 'Under the incorrect name of cod tripe, the pneumatic or swimming bladders are also prepared: these consist of a bag of air, seven to eight inches long and three or four wide, attached to the concavity of the thick spine of the fish from the front to the rear. This bladder is thick and of a jelly-like substance'.

Today it is one of the most valued parts of the cod, especially in the popular seafood cookery of Catalonia, although in recent times it has beneficially infused much of Spain's renowned cuisine. And in some places its aggressive name has been sweetened by calling it 'cod tripe' because of its similar texture to that of land animals, and even 'gelatineous curls', as the Navarro chef Koldo Rodero called it to reduce fear in his menu long ago.

There are popular Catalan recipes that guarantee its importance, such as the unforgettable cod tripe, stewed with the jewel of a vegetable, Ganxet beans. And in the haute cuisine of the author, we can identify dishes of substance such as 'Senia Rice' with *socarrat,* charred cod skin and tripe with cauliflower buds, or the similarly charred work of Quique Dacosta of El Poblet in Denia, and that of another great creator Andoni Luis Adúriz, who delighted us some time ago with his 'Boiled Cheek and Cod Tripe, Sopakos, Tomatoes and Spicy Parsley Pistou'. A flavourful and unforgettable Mediterranean trip to the Bay of Biscay.

I

ts taste enchants

Cod and chilli

For the cod tripe

100 g salt cod tripe
olive oil, for frying

For the chilli and potato

1 potato, cooked and peeled
8 green chillies in vinegar
40 g cream cheese
20 g olive oil
chopped parsley
salt
ginger

In addition

pansy petals

4 people

method

For the cod tripe

Leave to soak in plenty of water for two
hours. Spread out to dry at 60°C for
approximately 12 hours. Set aside.
Cut into small pieces and fry in abundant
hot oil.

For the chilli and potato

Drain the chillies thoroughly and cut them
into thin rings.
Mash the potato with a fork to make a
purée. Add the remaining ingredients.
Season and add a pinch of ginger.

Arrange the fried tripe, stuffed, if
the gut permits, or smeared with
the chilli and potato preparation.
At the last moment, add the
pansy petals.

The third spice

This spice has a long history, and was used by the early Egyptians and later by the Greeks and Romans. It was carried to Europe along the ancient caravan routes and is the third most expensive spice, after saffron and vanilla, although it is used in such small amounts that we should not fear buying it unless we want to appear like the miser in the joke about the 'parrot's chocolate'.

Cardamom is widely used in India and the Middle East, but it is also an ingredient in cakes and pastries in Germany, Russia and Scandinavia. In France and the United States the essential oil is used in perfumes.

The plant grows profusely on the coast of Malabar in India, and other varieties are grown in Sri

Green cardamom pods are the most common, and the white ones are simply green pods that have been bleached. Avoid brown cardamom, as their taste is very unpleasant and reminiscent of the camphor placed in cabinets to protect clothes from moths.

For best results, the aromatic seeds should be removed from the green or white pods immediately before use.

Cardamom works well in pies, cakes, liquors, coffee, pickles, pickled herring, meat dishes, punches, spiced wine, custard and fruit dishes. And it is one of the components of a curry.

The seeds, whole or ground, lose their flavour quickly, so it is best to buy whole pods. You must remove the seeds from the pods before grinding them. For savoury dishes, dry toast the seeds to extract the best flavour. Open the pod and remove the sticky blackish brown seeds, heat up a frying pan, add the seeds and roast them.

Lanka, Mexico and Guatemala. It is a member of the pervasive ginger family, and is a perennial shrub of a certain height, with lanceolate leaves and short flower stems. After flowering, the stems form small green capsules that are harvested by hand; these capsules can contain up to 20 aromatic seeds.

An infusion of cardamom pods after dinner is not only refreshing and delicious, but also a good digestive. In the Middle East, strong black coffee is often flavoured with a pinch of cardamom powder. To prepare an infusion, place 12 crushed pods in 1.5 litres of boiling water, add a piece of orange peel and leave to rest for 10 minutes. Then add 2-3 tablespoons of tea, leave to gain the desired strength, strain and serve with hot milk and sugar, if you wish.

Coated hazelnut liquid

ingredients

4 people

For the hazelnut fritter

50 g almonds, fried with salt
375 g water
40 g hazelnut paste
125 g sugar
30 g balsamic vinegar cream
5 g xanthan gum

For the outside of the fritter

500 ml water
1 g chopped sage leaves
25 g natural gelatine, powdered
1 sheet gelatine (2 g per serving)

For the raspberry veil

20 g agar agar
20 g raspberries
10 g icing sugar

For the red reduction

250 ml water
100 g strawberries
1 g ground black pepper
130 g sugar
1 g cardamom
½ g safflower

For the crisp biscuit

100 g egg yolk
150 g orange juice
2 egg whites
120 g icing sugar
50 g ground walnut
50 g ground almond
4 g ground cardamom
25 g flour

In addition

walnut chunks
puffed rice
black sesame crackers

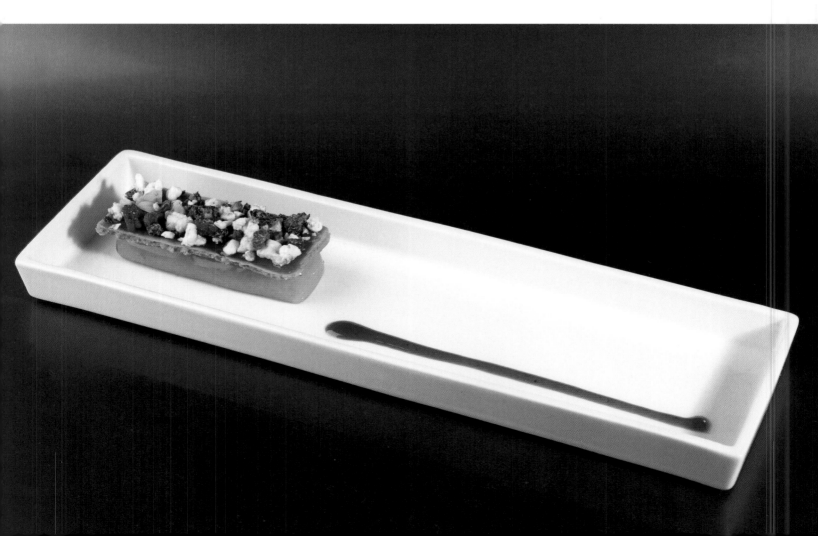

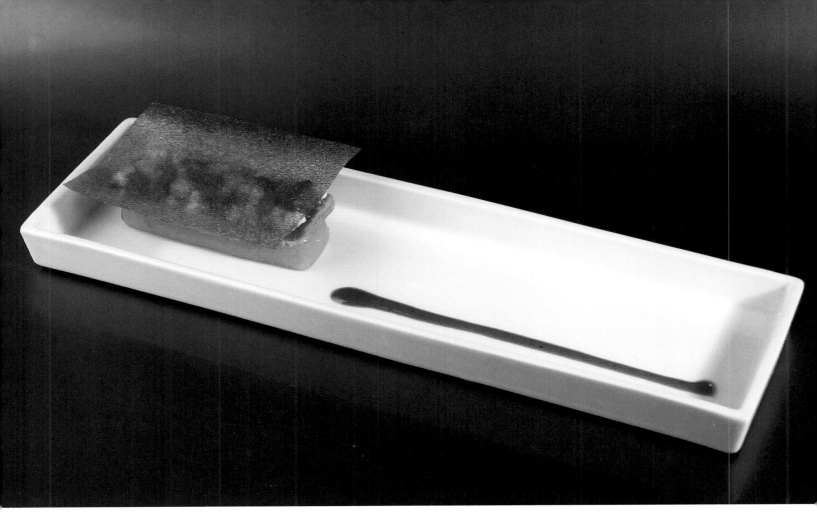

method

For the hazelnut fritter

Mix everything together and bring to the boil. Blend and strain. Place the mixture in a narrow rectangular flexipan mould and freeze.

For the outside of the fritter

Moisten the gelatine sheet well. Then boil for 20 seconds. Set aside at between 50-60°C.

For the raspberry veil

Mix all the ingredients and grind to a powder.
Grease a plastic mould about 20 cm long and 10 cm wide. Sprinkle the powder and shake the pan so that it spreads all over.
Boil the mould upside down in a pressurised steam oven at 119°C for 15 seconds.
Remove the veil adhering to the mould.

For the red reduction

Boil the ingredients. Drain and leave to reduce to a thick consistency.

For the crispy biscuit

Beat the egg yolks. Set aside.
Meanwhile, mix the orange juice with the egg whites and icing sugar. Once they are well incorporated, mix in the yolks.
Separately, mix the walnuts, almonds, cardamom and flour and add this mixture to the mixture of whites and yolks.
Spread this cream over a plate, forming a thin layer, and bake at 180°C for 7 minutes.
When cooked, cut into rectangles 7 x 3 cm. Set aside.

Hold a hazelnut fritter with two needles and place it in the gelatine mixture to form the outside of the fritter. Leave to rest for a moment and repeat the operation. Place on a tray, remove the needles and wait until the inside is liquid.
Place the crispy biscuit over it, and above this, the nut pieces, puffed rice and sesame crackers. Place the raspberry veil over them. Place the whole thing on a plate and spread the red reduction beside it.

The purifying bonfire

Although it may sound strange, ash can be a very interesting culinary condiment, and not altogether alien to tradition. We have been investigating this for some years, both in a theoretical and purely practical way. On the one hand, searching for references to ash in gastronomy and, on the other hand, accidentally, when ash formed after a product became burnt and blackened.

The historical references are from different cultures and countries around the world.

In Catalonia, the dish *calçots*, literally blackened, covered in ash, is a pure delight and very popular.

Its feast, the *calçotada*, is associated with Vals, a Catalan town to the north of the capital Tarragona. This fun festival and popular feast is a ritual established around a unique grill. *Calçots* – spring onions – are placed on the grill one hour before serving, then wrapped in newspaper and plastic to conserve their heat, so that they are soft and the completely scorched layer comes off with relative ease. Finally, they are served at the table piled up in the hollow of a rustic clay tile to keep them warm.

Our French neighbours still use ash in the production of certain cheeses, by covering them with ash, and our Mexican compadres make their moles with burnt garlic.

For our first recipe on this theme – already a few years old – and well known, Sea Bass in Leek Ash, we carried out many laboratory tests and, of all the foods we burned, what we liked best was leek. The preparation is easy, but we needed a good grill. The leeks are washed and placed on a rack over a grill until completely burnt. The burnt leeks are pulled apart and crushed with olive oil and other seasonings.

This ash sauce is poured through a cheese cloth, and is ready to use. It tastes of leek but you mustn't use too much of it. We use it to accompany sea bass, usually adding a droplet or a small line of this black sauce. In a new recipe with the expressive title Firebrands, the ash is aubergine (eggplant) and, in homage to ancestral fire, branches of unique black toasts are simulated as firebrands.

firebrands

ingredients

4 people

For inside the firebrand

220 g day-old bread
100 g cream
400 g milk
125 g sugar
1 vanilla pod

For outside of the firebrand

10 g aubergine ash
200 g cocoa butter

For the zahareña juice

100 g olive oil
2 g zahareña powder (*Sideritis incana*)

For the sweet zahareña

80 g zahareña
20 g sugar

For the branches of the 'bonfire'

180 g sugar
4 soup spoons water
pinch of zahareña powder

method

For inside the firebrand

First, remove the crusts from the bread and cut the dough into rectangles. Place them in a deep bowl. Boil the milk with the cream, sugar and vanilla. Then pour the mixture over the bread and leave to stand in the fridge for 24 hours.
Drain slightly and place in the freezer to harden into a block. Cut in the shape of firebrands, as suggested by the title, and store in the freezer until ready to use.

For outside the firebrand

Chop the cocoa butter and heat to no more than 50°C. Add the ash and mix, without letting the butter lose temperature.
Hold the firebrands with two hypodermic needles and bathe them in the mixture. Remove the needles and store the firebrands in the fridge.

For zahareña juice

Cold mix both ingredients.

For the sweet zahareña

Blend both ingredients to get a sweet powder.

For the branches of the 'bonfire'

Heat the sugar with water to 160°C and, with a fork, spread the caramel on parchment paper. As you spread it on the paper, sprinkle with a little zahareña.

Arrange the firebrands in the middle of the plate and sprinkle around the sweet zahareña. Add a little oil and place the bonfire between the firebrands.

The squaring of the circle?

It has been stated quite rightly that the school kitchen, where children are taught to cook, as well as being a fundamental learning for life – especially for those whose vocation will later lead them to become professionals of the stove – is also a great source of mathematical inspiration. Shaping dough for cookies or pasta (one of the first things taught) can be oriented to highlight geometric shapes. Working the dough to make rectangular, round, square pasta, to make balls then spheres, cylinders (little logs), using pastry cutters to form the dough into various shapes, knives (which can be plastic) to cut triangular cookies – these are all activities for younger children that can incorporate the technical language of geometry and which, in addition, with trial and error, and by comparing end results, will gradually build up basic geometric ideas.

This is one aspect of geometry in early childhood. But at the professional level, what is important is not only the beautiful and evocative presentation of each dish but also the personal touch presented in geometric form by the containers used (the countless shapes of plates, rectangular, oval, square or round in current tableware) and also in the contents.

In the communication of daily cookery, there are influences that are linked to geometry in various ways. On the one hand, geometry plays an important role in the technical aspects of preparing a dish: Sometimes this arises naturally from the form of the raw materials themselves or the need to take advantage of specific parts with specific geometry. In other cases, the geometric components of a dish can be imposed by the need to expand the outward appearance of the material to be cooked, both for better use of its constituents and for better interaction with the taste buds. And in almost all cases, in its final presentation, the design of a dish must always play with shapes and colours that convey more.

At this final stage, objective influences are involved, art, communication and contemporary culture itself, adapted by the subjectivity of taste and the sensitivity of the cook; also conveying the groundbreaking concept of subverting reality, essentially turning a squid into an empty circle or a round-shaped apple into a square. The squaring of the circle?

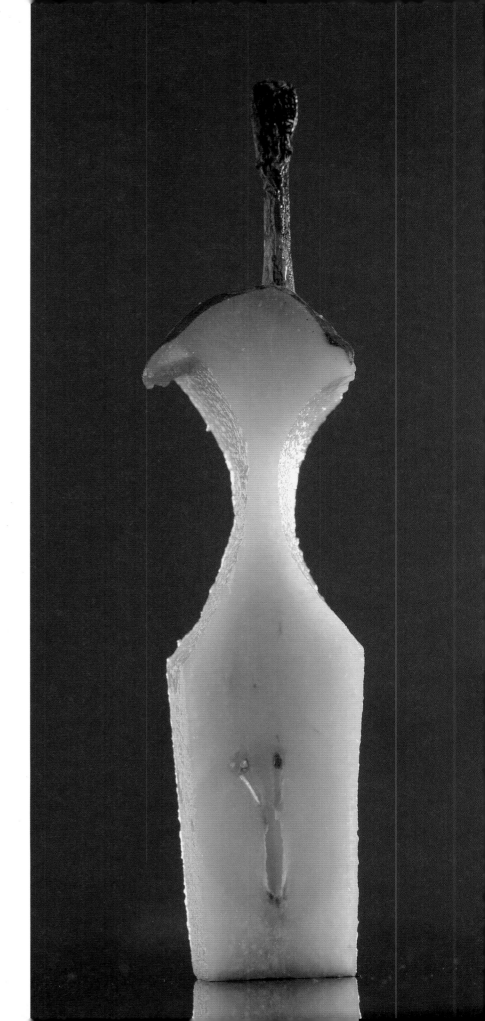

The square apple

ingredients

4 people

For the interior of the square apple

800 g apple peel and cores (keep the apple
   pulp for another dish)
50 g sugar
80 g cider
4 macadamia nuts
salt
pepper

For the outside of the apple

300 g cocoa butter
2 g dry parsley powder
5 g freeze-dried apple

For the white sheet

125 g white chocolate
1 g sweet paprika
1.5 g tandoori masala powder

For the gin and apple stock

100 g apple juice (without straining)
25 g gin
3 g rice vinegar
25 g sugar

For the sweet milk

1 can condensed milk
100 g milk
1 g rosemary
10 g Pennyroyal

In addition

pansy petals and olive oil

method

For the interior of the square apple

Heat the oven to 170°C. Boil the apple peel and cores with the sugar and cider for an hour. Pass through a sieve to make a purée. Season lightly and pour into a cube-shaped mould; insert a nut into each cube. Freeze them. Once frozen, remove from the moulds and store in the freezer until used.

For the outside of the apple

Melt the cocoa butter up to, but no more than, 50°C. Add the apple and parsley. Using a hypodermic needle, dip the frozen apple cubes in this to form a thin film. Leave to stand in the refrigerator.

For the white sheet

Melt the white chocolate and spread it in a thin layer on a plastic sheet. Sprinkle the mixture of paprika and tandoori powder over the chocolate. Once cold, remove the sheets from the plastic and keep them in the refrigerator.

For the gin and apple stock

Blend the ingredients and set aside.

For the sweet milk

Bring a pan of water to the boil and cook the tin of condensed milk for 30 minutes.
Make an infusion with the milk, rosemary and Pennyroyal, as if it were tea. Strain and mix with the condensed milk at a ratio of 150 g infusion to 45 g milk.

Arrange the apple on a shallow plate and place a pansy on it. In front of it, the white sheet, heated slightly. Drizzle the sweet milk and the gin and apple stock around it. Garnish with a few pansy petals and a little oil.

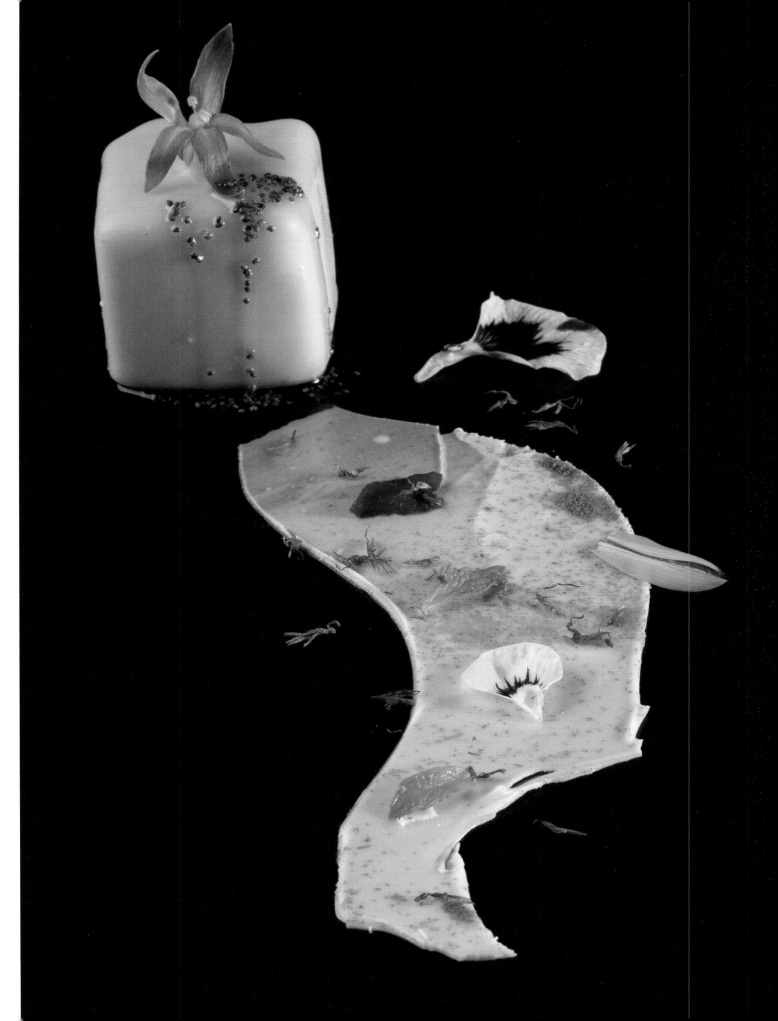

The squid circle

ingredients

4 people

For squid a la plancha and chopped raw squid

1 large squid (*begi haundi*)
2 tablespoons garlic oil
8 g orange peel, dried and ground
ginger
chopped parsley
sarsaparilla powder
salt

For the bed of vegetables and squid

1 large onion
1 green pepper
1 clove garlic
2 tablespoons olive oil
tentacles and wings of the squid
1 green plum, diced
sarsaparilla powder
ginger
salt

For the sauce

100 g lightly sautéed onion
100 g chicken broth
1.5 g bergamot tea
5 g soy sauce
salt
sugar

For the reduction of cocoa and ginger

50 g water
1.5 g cocoa powder
15 g sugar
5 g balsamic vinegar
1 g ground ginger

method

For squid a la plancha and chopped raw squid

Clean the squid and separate the fins and tentacles to one side and the body to another.
Open the body in half and cut it into large fillets (9 x 9 cm). Make a few holes in the squid with a pastry cutter 1.5 cm in diameter. Save the leftover circles.
Marinate the fillets in the garlic oil, salt, orange, ginger, chopped parsley, and sarsaparilla powder for 12 hours.
Cook the squid fillets a la plancha until they acquire a pretty colour.
Chop the circles of squid, add a pinch of parsley, salt, sarsaparilla powder and olive oil. Reserve them raw as the tartar.

For the bed of vegetables and squid

Clean and cut the vegetables into thin strips. Gently sauté the vegetables with the olive oil. When well done, add the tentacles and fins. At the last moment, add the diced plum. Season with sarsaparilla powder, ginger and salt.

For the sauce

Boil the broth with the onion. Blend and strain. Bring to the boil again. When it boils, remove from heat and add the tea. Leave to infuse for 5 minutes.
Add soy sauce, season and add a pinch of sugar.

For the reduction of cocoa and ginger

Boil everything and reduce by a quarter.

In the centre of the plate, place a small bed of vegetables and squid. Then stand the squid fillets upright against each other, so that the holes are correctly displayed. Spread the sauce underneath and draw a small line of the reduction on it. Arrange the tartar beneath.

Green, how I love you green

Chlorophyll has many beneficial qualities. It is a stimulant, depurative and anti-carcinogen. And once absorbed by the blood via the lymphatic system, this green pigment in plants, whose structure is very similar to our hemoglobin, activates cell metabolism, detoxifies, improving defence, the regenerative capacity of cells and their breathing power, natural healing processes, stimulates the formation of red blood cells, and helps to heal wounds. It cleanses the blood, stops infections, balances the acid-base ratio and prevents cancer, as noted by Laura Jimeno Muñoz, a great specialist on the subject, who described it very accurately as 'green blood'.

Its name comes from the Greek *khloros* – which means light green or yellowish green – and *phylon*, meaning 'leaf'.

Although it may seem strange, chlorophyll was not discovered until the beginning of the 19th century (in historical terms, two days ago) by the French chemists Pierre Joseph Pelletier and Joseph Bienaimé Caventou.

It is a plant pigment, present in all plants, fundamental to life on Earth because it is responsible for absorbing photons of light to perform photosynthesis. This process transforms light energy into chemical energy, creating oxygen that is released into the atmosphere for the benefit of all living beings on the planet.

It seems that the earliest forms of life able to convert solar energy into energy for life appeared on the Earth more than 3,600 million years ago and their successful nutrition and respiration systems have not changed since then. But it was not until 1913 that the transcendental functions of chlorophyll were discovered. The finding is due to Dr. Richard Willstätter, a German chemical engineer awarded the Nobel Prize for Chemistry in 1915 for his research in the field of vegetable colours.

Then in the 1960s Dr. H. E. Kirschner – who collected his interesting findings in the book *Nature's Healing Grasses* – stated specifically that 'chlorophyll is healing and powerful. Devastating to germs and viruses but gentle with diseased body organs and tissues, the way it works is nature's secret. It seems like green magic.'

Subsequently, Dr. Birscher, a physicist scholar of plant dyes, called chlorophyll the 'concentrated power of the Sun'.

Bonito with greens

ingredients

4 people

For the bonito loin

15 g dried black olives
400 g bonito
250 g coarse salt
olive oil 0.4 °

For the coffee oil, paprika...

100 g olive oil
30 g dried black olives
2 g soluble coffee
4 g sweet paprika
salt
icing sugar

For the salad and green vinaigrette

arugula, red chard, lamb's lettuce
200 g olive oil
5 g barley powder
10 g rice vinegar
5 g green barley juice (you can buy it ready-made)
salt
black pepper

For the potato

1 large potato
10 g barley powder
10 g green barley juice (you can buy it ready-made)
100 g olive oil
salt

method

For the bonito loin

To prepare the olives, stone and dehydrate them at 60°C.
Cut the loin into 1.5 cm slices and place in the coarse salt for 10 minutes. Then remove from the salt and place in the oil until used. When ready to serve, lightly grill the fish smeared with the crushed olives. Set aside.

For the coffee oil, paprika...

Mix all the ingredients. Add salt.

For the salad and green vinaigrette

Mix all the vinaigrette ingredients, except the arugula, lamb's lettuce and red chard. Add these to the vinaigrette dressing at the last minute. Set aside.
To make the green barley juice extraction, introduce the green barley leaves into a mixture of equal proportions of water and ethyl alcohol 96°. Leave to stand at 50°C for 2 hours. Then raise the temperature to 75°C so that the alcohol evaporates. Strain to remove the leaves.

For the potato

Cook the potato, wrapped in greaseproof paper in the microwave for about 5-7 minutes. Once cooked, peel it and cut it into rectangles. Season with the mixture of the rest of the ingredients. Set aside.

Place the rectangle of potato on a flat plate. Place the bonito on it. Over that, the salad dressed with the vinaigrette, pile it high and with all the stems to one side. In front of it all, paint a few brushstrokes of coffee oil. To one side of the salad drizzle a trace of vinaigrette.

Metamorphosis

As my daughter Elena and our research team (Xabi Gutiérrez and Igor Zalakaín) explained in detail at Madrid Fusion 2009, colour can be both the star and the most innovative element of a dish.

Creative cooks use colour schemes in their dishes to portray which colours inspire, for example, the freshness and naturalness of green, the warmth of orange or the vitality and strength of red.

One example of colour as an extra flavour is the recipe Bonito Parterre. A parterre is a garden with flowerbeds or bordered plants, generally in a symmetric design. And so it is in this dish: with smoked bonito in plants or soil. The triangles are the green of leeks, cooked for barely two minutes to retain their colour, then worked to resemble a thin sheet of paper, simulating the parterre grass. And the vivid reddish part (the so-called flowers) in this hypothetical garden are made using cochineal, *Dactylopius coccus*, also known as carmine cochineal. A bug converted to a flower.

Cochineal is an insect, originally from Mexico, which feeds on the sap of the cactus or prickly pear and, as a defence, the female produces a red liquid, which is used as a dye.

There is evidence that this pigment was used in Peru and Mexico, prior to the Spanish conquest. In Aztec Mexico it was used to colour textiles. According to Friar Bernardino de Sahagún, who aptly describes it in his *General History of Things of New Spain* (a work of 1569, which remained unpublished until 1829), it was called *nocheztli*, which means 'prickly pear blood because in some genres of prickly pear, worms called mealybugs are bred, attached to the leaves, and these worms have very red blood'. The first shipment of cochineal to Europe occurred in 1523, and for several centuries cochineal was, along with gold and silver, one of the most valuable materials exported from America. But the truth is that until recently it was used exclusively as a textile dye.

Bonito parterre

ingredients

4 people

For the bonito sauce

30 g bread
1 g cochineal
juice of half a lemon
100 g olive oil 0.4 °
30 g fried sunflower seeds
30 g bitters
2 chopped mint leaves
salt
pinch of sugar

For the bonito fillets

500 g bonito (125 g per serving)
salt
ginger

For the cochineal sauce

0.2 g cochineal
100 g olive oil 0.4 °
5 g sugar
0.5 g xanthan gum
salt

For the cochineal parterre

500 g bonito broth
25 g vegetable gelatine
2 g agar agar
1 g cochineal
salt
ginger

For the green parterre

the green part of 3 leeks
water
salt

In addition

various flowers of different colours
salt flakes

method

For the bonito sauce

Mix all the ingredients, crush and season.

For the bonito fillets

Cut the bonito loins in rectangles (2 pieces per serving). Lightly smoke them for 4 minutes in a smoker. Once completed, season and add a pinch of ginger. Coat with the sauce and quickly cook a la plancha, leaving them juicy.

For the cochineal sauce

Crush everything well. Lightly boil, strain and season.

For the cochineal parterre

For the bonito broth (1 litre of water, 1 leek, 200 g of bonito cuttings, salt, powdered ginger), cook over low heat for one hour. Strain and add a pinch of salt and ginger. Cold mix all ingredients and boil them. Spread over a very thin plastic sheet. Once gelled, cut into circular wafers. Reserve them on parchment paper until used.

For the green parterre

Cut the leeks into thick slices and cook them in water with a pinch of salt. Once cooked, place in the Thermomix and crush for a moment, forming a thick fibrous or spun purée. Spread the mixture in a thin layer on paper and allow to dry at 60°C. Once dry, cut into triangular slices. Make them shine with a brush of oil before serving.

Arrange the bonito fillets splattered with salt flakes and drizzle with the cochineal sauce. At the side, place the circular and triangular parterres. Decorate with various flowers and herbs.

Crystal clear

I sincerely believe that most contemporary cookery seeks something more than taste and visual satisfaction, just as haute cuisine and confectionery has been doing for a long time. Today Carême's eighteen culinary constructions may seem very grandiose but in his day they had a great impact, and came as a surprise to the most seasoned gourmets of the time. Currently, as a plus to the inventiveness of culinary creations, the same idea is being pursued more vigorously, since, although it may seem that nothing is new, we have to maintain both actively and passively the intention to surprise, and the desire to be surprised. Some time ago, with the evocative and magical title Disappearances, we opened a chapter of recipes that almost makes us magicians, using succulent tricks that, far from being secret, we have made public.

The inspiration for this topic arose some time ago in one of the best-known creations that certainly stunned more than one person. It is 'Mutant Soup'. Despite its name, it is not, of course, a work of science fiction, but a delight for the palate and, above all, a pleasant surprise. It would arrive at the table in a bowl, where a few small black bundles (coated in squid ink jelly) later revealed slices of pumpkin within, themselves filled with strips of squid and vegetables. The waitress poured a transparent broth of baby squid and lime over the black 'packets'. As soon as the broth touched the bundles, the orange pumpkin was revealed and the transparent broth transformed into a black stock. Despite seeming very modern, this cannot really be called whimsical or quirky, as there have been all kinds of curiosities in the history of soups and stocks, not only in oriental, but also in some European cookery.

A more recent surprise of this kind is a dessert called Intxaursaltsa with Mutant Red Cabbage. Its striking name is due to the broth which changes colour because of the vegetable at the base of the dish.

In the gestation of this recipe, there was also something very surprising, inspired by the discovery that a drop of a washing-up liquid on a greasy plate, looked like it had 'eaten' it, and the plate (or pan) changed colour. This mutation was achieved by the addition of an ingredient with a different pH. If you add a few drops of lemon juice, egg white, tangerine juice or bicarbonate to red cabbage broth, the broth changes colour, becoming more pink or more violet, depending on the pH that it possesses.

The disappearance

ingredients

4 people

For the amaranth and olive cake

70 g amaranth
25 g olive oil
125 g egg whites
80 g sugar
80 g egg yolks

For the crunch

100 g sunflower seeds, peeled
70 g sugar

For the acid fruit juice

100 g water
50 g passion fruit
60 g sugar
15 g pink grapefruit

For the black ball

20 g sugar
2 g coffee powder
2 g desalinated aubergine ash

method

For the amaranth and olive cake

Toast the amaranth and crush it finely with the oil. Mix with the other ingredients and sieve them. Insert into a siphon and give it 2 charges. Set aside.

For the crunch

Toast the seeds with the sugar in a pan. Leave to cool and set aside.

For the acid fruit juice

Cold mix the ingredients. Set them aside.

For the black ball

Using a machine for making candy floss, pour in the sugar until it becomes a thread. Pick it up and form a ball. Smear it with the other ingredients. Set aside.

Bake the sponge cake left in the siphon in the microwave for 25 seconds at maximum power, filling one third of the volume of a 125 ml disposable plastic cup.
Remove and place it to one side of the plate, above the crunchy seeds. In the middle, place the acid fruit juice.
Present it to the diner like this. In front of him, the ball will disappear within three seconds, giving a special touch to the broth.

intxaursaltsa with mutant red cabbage

ingredients

4 people

For the cabbage broth

65 g chopped cabbage
250 g water
10 g sugar

For the liquefied cabbage

100 g chopped cabbage
water

For intxaursaltsa

500 ml cream
1 coffee spoon ground cinnamon
250 g chopped walnuts
150 g icing sugar

For the intxaursaltsa bath

400 g water
100 g port
25 g vegetable gelatine
2 g cochineal

For the fried chestnuts

60 g chestnuts
frying oil
salt
nutmeg
powdered star anise

In addition

40 g demerara sugar
juice of 1 lemon
8 sugared walnuts

method

For the cabbage broth

Boil the water with sugar. Add the chopped cabbage and cook for 2 minutes. Strain and save for other uses; reserve the broth only.

For the liquefied cabbage

Blanch the cabbage in boiling water. Drain and run it through a blender. Reserve the juice (about 90 g).

For intxaursaltsa

Cook all the ingredients in a saucepan over low heat for about 18 minutes. Pour the intxaursaltsa into rectangular moulds and freeze. Once frozen, cut into small triangles. Keep in the freezer until ready to use.

For the intxaursaltsa bath

Boil all the ingredients for 2 minutes. Bathe the frozen pieces of intxaursaltsa, with the help of a hypodermic needle, just until a red skin forms on the outside. Leave to rest.

For the fried chestnuts

Peel the chestnuts and cut them into thin slices, fry them in hot oil to make fine chips. Season lightly and sprinkle with salt, nutmeg and powdered anise.

To prepare the cabbage juice: mix 125 g broth, 50 g liquefied cabbage and 1 coffee spoon of demerara sugar. Arrange the bathed triangles of intxaursaltsa on a plate, place a few chestnut chips over them and some chopped sugared walnuts. Drizzle with the cabbage juice. At the last moment pour over the lemon juice, so that it totally changes the colour of the sauce.

From necessity...

Prior to smoking, drying is one of the oldest methods of food preservation, requiring the application of heat.

All grains and cereals are preserved by drying. Some fruits and vegetables are also preserved this way, which is very useful because drying requires little human effort, when performed naturally. Throughout history, dehydration has been one of the most widely used techniques for the conservation of food. As early as Paleolithic times, about a whopping 400,000 years ago, people were sun-drying foods, such as fruits, grains, vegetables, meat and fish, as they learnt – of course with many failures and errors – how to subsist in times of basic food shortage. This principal conservation technique aims to preserve the quality of food by lowering water activity and reducing moisture content, thereby avoiding deterioration and microbiological contamination during storage.

Several methods of dehydration can be used, or a combination of them all, such as solar drying, hot air, microwave, atomization, osmotic dehydration, among others... However, for dehydrated food to be of good quality, it is essential to study in detail the phenomena of transfer of matter and energy involved in the process, such as changes to structure (porosity, firmness, shrinkage, density) and biochemical reactions (oxidation, enzymatic, non-enzymatic, denaturation).

The use of heat to dry food was practiced by many people of the New and Old World. But it was not until 1795 that hot air dehydration was invented (at 105°F) on thin slices of vegetables. Dehydration involves control over climatic conditions in the chamber or circulating micro-environmental control.

... to pleasure

But although this technique was born out of necessity, today, in many cases, it is used for pure pleasure, as other more sophisticated and improved media (freeze-dried, frozen and vacuum-packed etc) can achieve more accomplished goals for the mere conservation of a product.

One of the prime examples of this is something that many people, especially the Italians, appreciate as a gastronomic pearl, the appetizing *stoccafisso* or stockfish (essential in the unique recipe for the famous *baccalà mantecato* or creamed dried cod), which is nothing other than *skrei* from Norway's Lofoten Islands, whole, naturally dried throughout the winter in so-called 'cathedrals', wooden pyramid structures, on whose bars they are hung in pairs, tied by the tail. This is without brine and very different from the usual salt cod. And in this jewel of *stoccafisso*, the combination of sun and cold air makes it an undeniably gustatory marvel.

Live seafood soup

ingredients

4 people

For the stock

2 onions
1 leek
1 shallot
15 g olive oil 0.4 °
15 g butter
500 ml clarified vegetable stock
0.2 g marshmallows

For the vegetables

½ green pepper
½ red pepper
30 g pumpkin
20 g green beans
20 g beetroot
10 g carrots

For the carabineros 'brains'

20 g carabineros 'brains'
10 g olive oil
0.5 g powdered tonka
salt
pepper

In addition

pinch of freeze-dried beetroot
2 tablespoons walnut oil

method

For the stock

Cut the vegetables into julienne and sauté gently in the oil and butter. Add the stock and bring to the boil. Infuse the marshmallow for 2 minutes, covered. Strain and reserve.

For the vegetables

Cut them very thinly and dehydrate at 55°C. Set aside.

For the carabineros 'brains'

Place the 'brains' in the oil and season with powdered tonka, salt and pepper. Leave for 10 minutes.

Place the carabineros 'brains', soaked in walnut oil, at the bottom of a small bowl or soup dish. Arrange strands of different dried vegetables over it and a little freeze-dried beetroot powder.
Take it to the table like this, accompanied by a small pitcher with the 'boiling' stock. Place the dish in front of the diner and pour just 100 ml of stock over it, and cover it with a transparent bell glass. After one minute, withdraw the glass cover, and the diner will smell the nuances retained in the glass, mainly tonka and marshmallow, with traces of seafood.

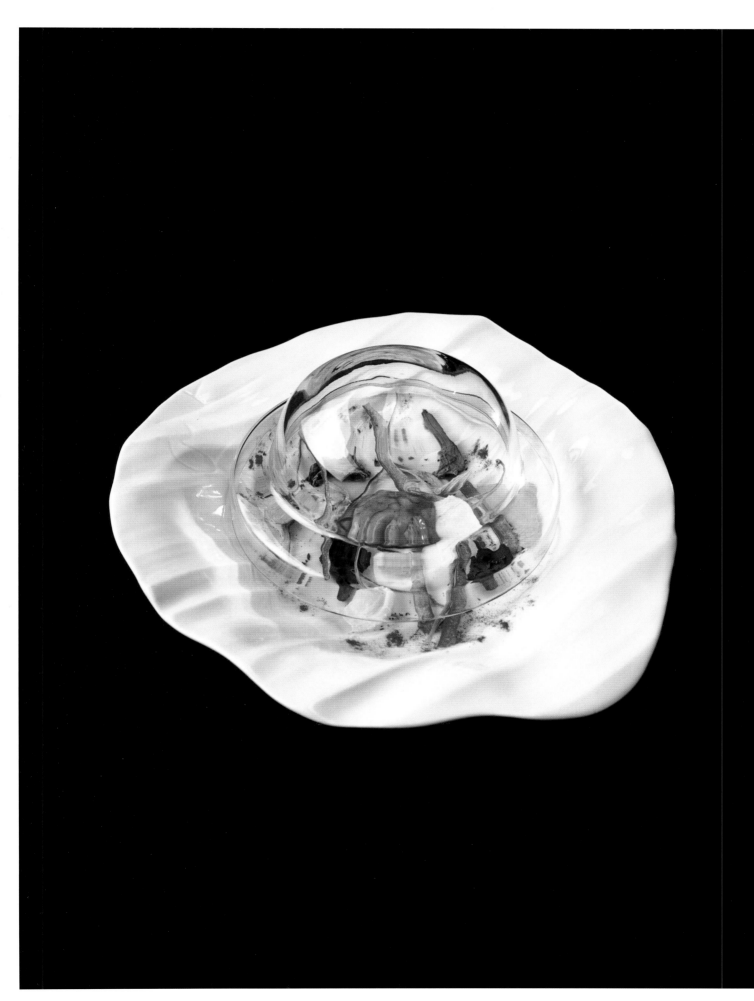

ingredients

4 people

For the hake

600 g hake loin/fillet (150 g per serving)
2 tablespoons olive oil
salt
powdered ham

For the salsa verde

3 cloves garlic, finely chopped
1 tablespoon chopped parsley
3 tablespoons olive oil 0'4°
50 g clams
250 ml cold water
salt

For porrusalda wafers

3 cleaned leeks
60 g peeled potato
40 g cleaned carrots
2 litres water
3 g kappa carrageenan (per 250 g mash)
salt

For the parsley and basil seeds

40 g parsley leaves
200 g olive oil
4 g basil seeds
25 g parsley juice
200 g water
1 g parsley seeds

In addition

Powdered rooibos tea

hake with seeds

method

For the hake

Clean the hake and cut into portions. Season and add a pinch of powdered ham.

For the salsa verde

Heat the very finely chopped garlic and half the chopped parsley in a saucepan over a low heat, in the oil. Before the garlic starts to brown, add a pinch of flour if you like. Season.
Then add the clams. Cover with water and cook for 5 minutes. Add the remaining parsley. Set aside.

For the porrusalda wafers

Cut the leeks, carrots and potatoes and cook them in water with a little salt. Mash to make a light purée. Add salt to taste.
For each 250 g of purée add 3 g of kappa. Blend and bring to the boil. Pour onto a plate. When cool, cut with a pastry cutter, 5 cm in diameter.

For the parsley and basil seeds

Thoroughly crush the parsley leaves with the oil. Strain.
Hydrate the basil seeds in the mixture of parsley juice and water for 5 minutes. Drain and place them in the parsley oil, along with the parsley seeds.

Cook the hake lightly, a la plancha, with a little oil. Finish cooking it in the salsa verde. Care must be taken to keep it very juicy.
Place the hake fillet on a plate and, at its side, the porrusalda wafer. Drizzle the seeds on the wafers and beside the hake. Sprinkle the hake lightly with rooibos.

The deer's footprints

ingredients

For the sauce

500 g deer bones
2 onions
1 garlic clove
250 ml water
250 ml venison stock
olive oil
1 g ground cardamom
salt
black pepper

For the venison

800 g rack of venison
salt
5 tablespoons olive oil
pepper

For the deer sauce

1 clove garlic, fried
20 g peeled sunflower seeds
40 g venison meat, sautéed
15 g orange liqueur
15 g pacharán
15 g gin
20 g toasted bread
4 chopped oregano leaves
salt
black pepper

For the deer's footprints

100 g dry bread
deer sauce
1 potato

For the salsify

2 salsify
50 g parsley juice
salt

method

For the sauce

Lightly brown the bones with a bit of oil. Add the garlic and the onions, cut into julienne strips, and sauté for a few minutes. Deglaze and moisten with the stock and the water. Simmer for 2 hours. Drain, season and add the cardamom. Set aside.

For the venison

Thoroughly clean the venison and cut into portions.
Coat the slices with sauce and brown well in oil on all sides. Add salt and pepper. Set aside.

For the deer sauce

Mix all the ingredients and crush together. Add salt and pepper.

For the deer's footprints

It is advisable to freeze the bread so that it cuts easily into pieces. Cut thin slices of bread and spread with the deer sauce. Dry the bread at 60°C. Once dry, reduce it to dust. Set aside.
Cut the potato in the shape of a deer's hoof.

For the salsify

Peel the salsify and cut into small pieces. Cook in salted water. Once cooked, drain and place in the parsley juice until ready for use.

Sprinkle the deer powder. 'Step' on it with the potato,
leaving two or three footprints. To one side, place the
venison, accompanied by the salsify. Lightly drizzle over
the venison.
Lightly drizzle some deer sauce over the venison.

With flowers again

Cooking with flowers is neither strange nor cutting edge. You just need to read through gastronomic literature to see that, in cookery, almost everything has already been done before. To discover that the use of flowers is as old as it is natural, just go back to classical antiquity and look at how the Romans perfumed their dishes. In Apicius's recipes, there is mention of rose petals, marjoram flowers in mincemeat, and sauces made from saffron-coloured safflowers, and even wine aromatized with roses or violets. He specifically speaks of rose cakes, scented and adorned with rose petals. The Romans were also fascinated by mallow flowers, and apparently Charlemagne loved them in salads, just as in the late medieval ages, tuberoses were the showy whim of several French kings in more than one dish.

A few centuries earlier, in *The Odyssey*, Homer speaks of a country whose inhabitants eat lotus flowers. A reference which isn't strange when you consider that these flowers have been used since time immemorial in Chinese cuisine, along with others, such as magnolia and jasmine. Similarly, delicate Japanese cuisine uses chrysanthemums, among other flowers, in certain dishes, especially at New Year, as well as in some salads in the last months of the year.

According to Eduardo Mendez Ries in his interesting *Gourmet Dictionary*, it was precisely these Japanese influences that Prosper Montagne, famous chef and scholar in Paris between the wars, 'imbibed', when he created Salade Francillon, which incorporates them.

In the Middle East and Far East, orange and rose blossoms have been used since ancient times, whereas the Mediterranean regions opted for pumpkin and zucchini flowers, both as starters and garnishes, stuffed, fried, etcetera.

In the Middle East dried rose buds are mostly used as condiments, and jams are made with rose petals. But it is in the Far East, as already mentioned, that flowers are most often involved in cookery itself. Chrysanthemum or magnolia petals are very common in salads, jasmine and hibiscus flowers with poultry and fish, and yellow lily is used to season sauces and soups, to give a few examples. Tuberoses are highly relevant in various specialities of Hindustani cookery, while in Indonesia jasmine flowers are used to flavour chicken and other poultry dishes. Rose petals 'reign' in countries like Algeria or Tunisia, where they

are widely used to perfume dishes like couscous or lamb stews. In our own Europe flowers are especially used in a flavouring drinks and liquors. Their role in salads is usually limited to a mainly decorative function, but butters are often found to be flavoured with jasmine petals, orange, lemon or garlic. Flowering mint holds a thousand charms with fish, as do lime flowers and jasmine, which can also be mixed with some stuffings. Wild violets are happily married to ox, savoury flowers with beef, sage with pork tripe, and mint and thyme with lamb. Another culinary flower, which we have already mentioned, is the zucchini, so fashionable among the Nice chefs back in the eighties, and a particular highlight of the then ground-breaking chef Jacques Maximin.

And in France, this is not the only flower that is important in gastronomy; others, such as violets, have also left their mark on preparations for trout, pigeons, various omelettes and versions of scrambled eggs, not to mention aromatic sorbets, while in the Midi peach flowers were used in delicious salads.

In Spain, those who think cooking with flowers is innovative need look no further than Andalusia and the cookery manuals of the chefs to the Spanish monarchs of the 16th and 17th centuries, to realize that, long ago, they were used comprehensively. There are countless references to candied rose petals, pastries stuffed with elderberry jam, wallflower liquor, meat flavoured with orange blossom flowers... Refined customs that two chefs Diego Granado and Francisco Martínez Montiño, echoed entirely. Today, examples are more specific and fewer but no less interesting, despite the fact that there are no limits. You must always ensure, by all means possible, that the flowers enhance the flavour of the main ingredient and never mask it. This is well known by Albert Adrià, renowned 'dessert chef', as he showed some time ago in his delightful book, *El Bulli Desserts*, with exciting examples like 'Iced Grapes with Hints of Flowers and Fruits', which included fascinating sugared roses. Using the same flower, he created the 'Sabayon of Roses and Rose Water Gelatine,' which accompanied a cinnamon ice cream with tangerine granita. A dessert which, as the author noted, has clear resonances with Morocco.

But when choosing flowers for cookery, you must be very careful. You must follow guidelines almost as stringent as those for mushrooms. First, only use edible flowers and make sure they have not been treated with pesticides. Beware! Florists flowers are very pretty but they may have been treated with chemicals. When in doubt as to whether a flower is edible or not, it is best to consult an expert on the subject. Also bear in mind that you have to pick them in the daytime and in dry weather, and only those that will be used at once. Wash them in cool water, remove the stamens, pistils and the white base of the petals; otherwise they will have a slightly bitter taste. Don't forget that some flowers like lavender, heather or roses can be dried for use out of season.

As for applications, some flowers are used because they provide delicate aromas and flavours. For example, lavender, rose petals, orange blossom and nasturtium often flavour things as disparate as sorbets, spirits, wines, teas, puddings, jams or jellies. Indeed, you can say that the nasturtium plant, native of Peru and initially known as Indian cress, is as culinary as pork or duck, in that every part is used. Its leaves, usually of a strong spicy flavour, are reminiscent of watercress, its flowers (yellow, orange, red or even a creamy colour) have a light fragrance and five long petals. Finally, the seeds are pickled like capers.

However, there are other flowers that are more appropriately decorative. This is the case with chrysanthemums, borage flowers, which are purple and very showy, variegated geraniums, and marigolds, which are yellow, and give beautiful colour to a salad, for example. But even if we say they are decorative, the sight of them also stimulates the palate and, therefore, they can arguably be said to give a remarkable taste sensation.

Consensual deception

Much has happened since the great writer and chef (to use a current term) Emilia Pardo Bazán bequeathed to us these prescient words, which perhaps we now understand better than ever: 'Every era of history modifies the stove, and every nation eats according to its soul, perhaps before its stomach.' This I believe may be relevant to the topic at hand, which is none other than form in cookery and its varied expression throughout history. Of course, this does not devalue one iota the importance of flavour and taste as the basis of good cooking, both in the past and now. Form cannot mask the real taste of what we eat. But it can turn a necessary act, a sometimes daily routine, such as mere nutrition, into a celebration of the senses. And the sense of sight is not the least important. Hence, we have created a number of recipes, within the margin of their indispensable palatability, to enhance the aspect of various kinds of form. Firstly we have, *trompe l'oeil* (performed in multiple cuisines in the world) to reflect a complex world of appearance and reality, impact and mystery, also very present in the seventh art, cinema, and of course, in painting and even architecture.

As its name suggests, the trompe-l'oeil – from the French – is nothing more than a trap for the eye, and the Spanish Royal Academy of language defines it as: ' A trap or illusion that deludes someone into seeing what is not.' In any case, it is a deception that always consists of a tasty and even complicit form. Because we already know that 'Pumice Stone', 'Sardine Fossil' or 'Foie Gras Totem' or 'The Moonstone' are the fruits of a chef's imagination, identifying his creative works with forms that originate in these statements and are reasonably similar to the real world.

The fractal theme needs an explanation, even though it is very elementary and succinct...

Science or, in this case mathematics, can be integrated into food in a natural form, as is the case with fractal food.

A fractal is a semi-geometric object whose basic structure, fragmented or irregular, is repeated in different scales. The term was invented not long ago, in 1975, by the mathematician Benoît Mandelbrot, and derives from the Latin fractus, meaning broken or fractured. Many natural structures are fractal. Clouds, mountains, the circulatory system or snowflakes are natural fractals.

The most representative food that Mother Nature offers is romanesco broccoli, a cross between broccoli and cauliflower, which has an hypnotic and recurring design. On other occasions fractal foods are forced by the creative hand of man, for example in the dish which interests us here, 'Fractal Venison'.

What is perhaps more daring is to call a dish by the name of the tool that performs its point-to-point visual implementation, the thermocut. First and foremost, it should be noted that this is a machine that cuts very accurately. The research team was visiting an engineering college and discovered this apparatus, which fascinated us. There it was used to cut material to build models. To us, it seemed perfect for making a few special cuts in fruits and vegetables. The filament is so fine, it allows us to make very amusing cuts (letters or drawings). We can cut fruits, vegetables and jellies just as we want them and then knock them out on the grill or in the oven, dry them or caramelise them.

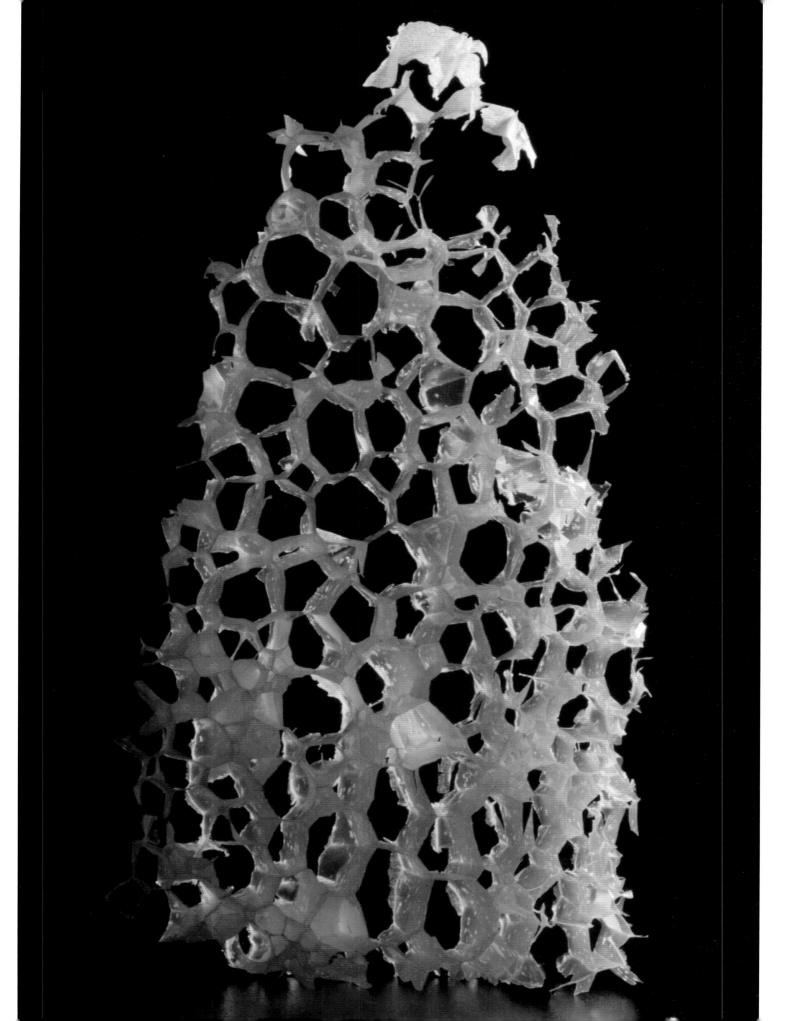

fractal venison

ingredients

4 people

For the venison

2 clean venison loins (4 servings of 130 g)
2 tablespoons olive oil

For the venison sauce

½ onion and ½ leek, well poached
30 g ketchup
50 g must (red wine)
50 g toast
50 g black olives
30 g olive oil
1 coffee spoon lemon juice
salt
black pepper
sugar

For the sauce

500 g venison bones
2 onions
1 clove garlic
250 ml water
250 ml vension stock
2 tablespoons olive juice
salt
black pepper

For the black olive sheet

200 g black olive broth
4.5 g kappa carrageenan
100 g water
15 g cocoa powder
15 g sugar

For the fractal

125 g icing sugar
50 g flour
15 g almond
50 g butter cream
25 g orange juice
20 g sugar
pinch aubergine (eggplant) ash

In addition

1 tablespoon balsamic vinegar

method

For the venison

Coat the pieces with the sauce and place in vacuum-sealed bags. Bake in the Roner at 58°C for 30 minutes. Then remove them from the device.
Brown in a pan with a dash of oil. Set aside.

For the venison sauce

Mix all the ingredients and crush to a paste. Add salt and sugar if necessary.

For the sauce

Colour the bones lightly with a dash of oil. Add garlic and julienned onions and sauté for a few minutes. Deglaze and cover with the stock and the water. Simmer for 2 hours. At the last moment, add the olive juice. Strain, season and set aside.

For the black olive sheet

Boil the black olive broth with 3 g of kappa. Meanwhile, boil the water with the cocoa and sugar. Add the remaining kappa and mix well to form a smooth sauce.
Pour the black olive broth onto a fine smooth plate to form a very thin layer and make a few stripes on the juice with the sauce. Cut into squares and set aside.

For the fractal

Mix all ingredients to form a dough. When mixed leave to rest in the refrigerator for 2 hours.
Make 4 balls and crush them between two silpats with a rolling pin to form a thin sheet. Bake at 190°C.

Place the venison to one side of the plate. Beside it place the olive juice sheet. Make a few drops with the balsamic vinegar. Place the fractal over the venison. The venison sauce is served separately in a gravy boat.

Pumice stone

ingredients

For the stone

500 g white chocolate
75 g cocoa butter
4 g aubergine (eggplant) ash

For the citronella broth

300 g water
5 g citronella
100 g sugar
pulp of a passion fruit
juice of one lime
zest of half a lime

In addition

safflower strands
aubergine (eggplant) ash

method

For the stone

Vacuum pack the chocolate with the butter and ash. Place the bag in the Roner so that all the contents melt at 41°C. When all has melted, insert the contents of the bag into a siphon, close and give it 2 charges.
Pour the contents into a rectangular flexipan mould leaving a gap of approx 85%. Leave to cool. Then using a knife form into round stones.

For the citronella broth

Infuse the citronella in boiling water. Cover and leave to stand for 5 minutes. Strain and add the remaining ingredients. Mix well and store in the refrigerator.

Rub the edge of a container (preferably transparent) with a little oil and attach the safflower strands and the ash to it. Pour in the citronella broth and place the stones inside so that they float.

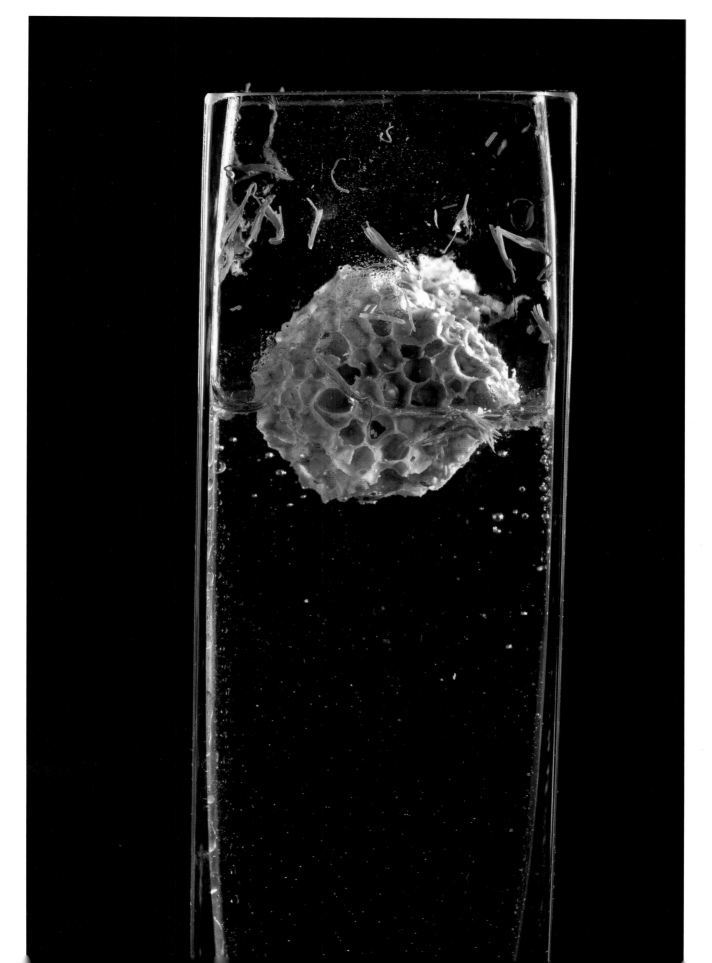

moonstone

ingredients

4 people

For inside the moonstone

480 g orange juice
4.8 g xanthan gum
50 g Cointreau liqueur
100 g sugar
liquid nitrogen

For outside the moonstone

50 g milk chocolate
200 g cocoa butter
60 g toasted breadcrumbs

Lunar dust

30 g toasted white sesame seeds
200 g sugar

For the thick red wine broth

100 g red wine
10 g soya
20 g sugar
0.5 g xanthan gum

In addition

pinch of powdered yuzu

method

For inside the moonstone

Mix the juice, xanthan gum, liqueur and sugar in a blender.
In a bowl containing liquid nitrogen, introduce a tablespoon of the mixture for 15 seconds, aiming to give it irregular shape. Remove the 'stone' and store in the freezer until ready to use.

For outside the moonstone

Melt the chocolate and butter up to 50°C. Add the breadcrumbs. Keep everything at the indicated temperature.
Using a hypodermic needle, dip the frozen stones into this to form an outer layer. Leave to rest. Store in the refrigerator.

Lunar dust

Grind both ingredients to powder.

For the thick red wine broth

Mix all the ingredients in the blender. Leave to rest to eliminate excess air.

Place 1 tablespoon of lunar dust on a matt black dish. Spread it around and, using a teaspoon, form three circles or craters of different sizes. Fill them with half a teaspoon of the thick red wine broth which, being very dark, will confuse, and appear to be empty. Place three stones around these craters. Sprinkle with a pinch of yuzu.

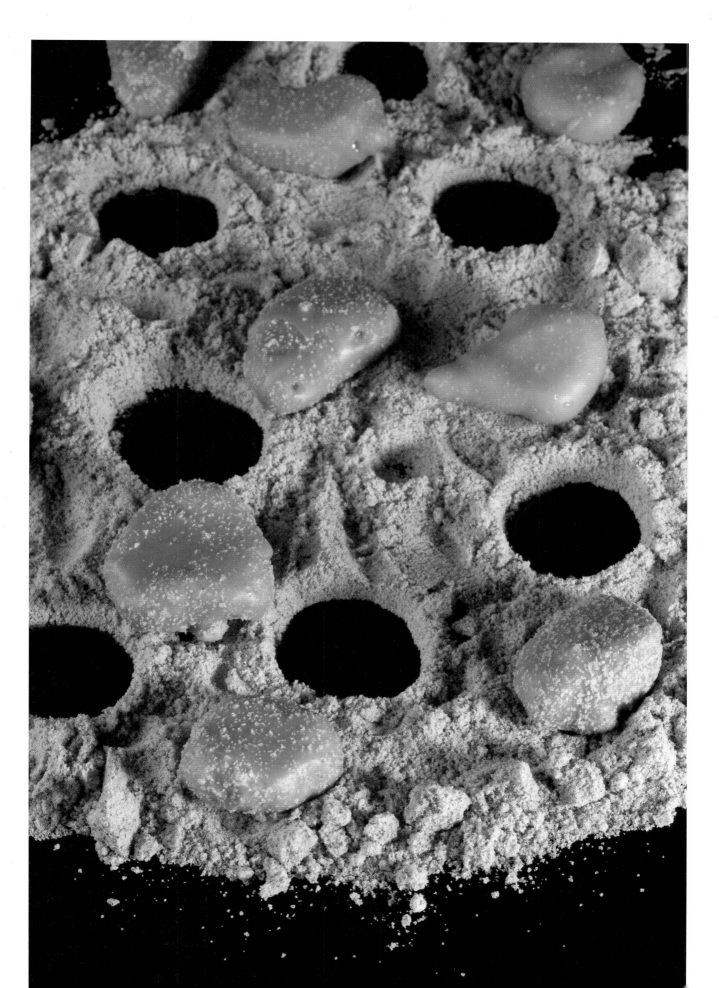

Sardine fossil

ingredients

4 people

For the sardine fossil

12 sardines
70 g soy sauce
30 g olive oil
15 g sugar
salt
pepper
ginger

For the arraitxikis preparation

200 g cleaned arraitxikis (erlas,
    muxarras, chicarrillos, karraspios,
    maidens, durdos etc.)
1 garlic clove
100 g fresh cheese
20 g soy sauce
chopped parsley
salt
pepper
ginger

For the green oil

half bunch of parsley
100 g spinach leaves
100 g olive oil
salt

method

For the sardine fossil

Clean the sardines and remove the tail,
head and guts. Coarsely crush them with
all the other ingredients so that pieces are
still visible. Add salt, pepper and a pinch
of ginger.
Roll out the dough between two sheets of
parchment paper and then fry it in oil (not
too hot) until golden. Drain the oil off well
and break the dough into 'fossils'.

For the arraitxikis preparation

Brown the chopped garlic in very little oil,
add the roughly chopped arraitxikis meat
and sauté everything. Remove, leave to
cool and add the remaining ingredients.
Add a pinch of ginger.

For the green oil

Blanch the parsley and spinach. Drain and
cool quickly. Crush and strain. Mix with
the oil until a really homogeneous mixture
is formed.
Season.

Place the arraitxikis mix on each fried 'fossil'. Accompany it with the green oil.

Foie gras 'totem'

ingredients

4 people

For the foie gras 'totem'

225 g duck foie gras (we use the leftover bits
   and pieces to prepare the escallops for the
   grilled foie gras dish)
salt
black pepper
nutmeg
chopped parsley
safflower

For the sweet love-in-a-mist

100 g sugar
50 g love-in-a-mist (*Nigella damascena*)
zest of half an orange

For the fenugreek vinaigrette

50 g olive oil
30 g grapefruit juice
1 g fenugreek powder (*Trigonella
   foenum graecum*)
10 g sugar
Salt

For the silver sheet

100 g white wine
50 g water
10 g sugar
0.5 g edible silver powder
1.5 g vegetable gelatine

In addition

chive shoots
safflower

method

For the foie gras 'totem'

Sauté the liver for a moment over high
heat. Season and add a pinch of pepper
and nutmeg. Place in irregular rectangular
flexipan moulds and allow to cool.
Unmould the foie gras and sprinkle with the
parsley and safflower.

For the sweet love-in-a-mist

Crush everything to a not-very-fine powder.
Set aside.

For the fenugreek vinaigrette

Cold mix the ingredients.

For the silver sheet

Cold mix and blend all the ingredients.
Bring to the boil and spread the mixture
thinly on to a sheet of non-stick paper. Cut
circles with a round pastry cutter.

Place the foie grois in the form of a 'totem' on a flat dish. Accompany it with the
sweet love-in-a-mist powder and fenugreek vinaigrette. Place two silver sheets
beside it. Garnish with the chive shoots and safflower.

Thermocut

ingredients

4 people

400 g water
5.5 g agar agar
280 g sugar
half stick of cinnamon
1 g gold dust
10 g glucose

method

Mix 100 g of water with the
agar agar. Bring to the boil
and add the remaining water,
sugar, cinnamon and gold
dust. Boil for 25 minutes over
low heat. Add the glucose and
boil for another 5 minutes.
Leave to gel in the fridge for
half an hour.
Once gelled, make artistic cuts
with the thermocut. Allow
to dry in the oven at 50°C
for 72 hours until a crispy
outer layer is formed and the
interior remains gelatinous.

Place on a black marble plate
and eat in one bite at room
temperature.

ingesting nature

It seems that European populations have traditionally made use of endless wild products, mostly various types of edible berries.

Civilization's advance sometimes produces effects that aren't always desirable. Thus, in Europe, the Romans brought with them the cerealization of food. The need to feed armies caused people to concentrate on raising crops, when harvesting in the forests, a few livestock and small gardens had been more than enough.

Forgotten until now but making a strong comeback in the heat of fashionable ecological trends, is something as wild and natural as berries.

Goji berries, of Asian origin, have only recently become known in the Western world. Their nutritional and medicinal properties have made them the latest fashionable foodstuff. They are highly valued for their colour and flavour, and can easily be grown at home.

Almost 2,000 years ago, goji berries were used as food and also therapeutically in traditional Chinese medicine. They are mentioned in a medical treatise of the 7th century Tang dynasty and in a *Compendium of Medical Terms* by Li Shizhen of the Ming dynasty, published in the 16th century. Their use is also widespread in traditional medicine in Korea, Japan, and Tibet. They taste slightly sweet, like dates, with a hint of something like tomato. They can be eaten raw, but it is considered healthier to use them in juice, marinated in wine, as an infusion or tincture. Goji berries belong to two shrub species of the family *Solanaceae* that are very close together: *Lycium barbarum* and *Lycium chinense*. Their exact origin is unknown, but it seems that they spread from southeast Europe to southwest Asia. These days, they grow in many regions of the world, especially in the British Isles, where they were introduced in the 18th century. Although they can be grown easily, even at home, and a single plant can produce more than one kilo of berries in its second year, China is the only country in which they are cultivated on a massive scale for commercial purposes. Since the beginning of the 21st century, goji berries have been introduced into Western markets, where until recently they were virtually unknown, becoming a trendy product praised by creative chefs and dietitians.

And in some ways, as it has been rightly said, behind the current culinary trends is 'a desire for the wild, to ingest the nature that was here before culture'.

ingredients

For the paste

200 g homemade tomato sauce
15 g Worcestershire sauce
5 g rooibos tea
50 g fried almonds
½ clove garlic fried
40 g hydrated goji berries (10 minutes in water)
3 tablespoons water
salt
pepper

For the pigeon

two baby pigeons (525 g each)
salt
ginger
liquorice

For the pigeon sauce

2 pigeon carcases
3 medium onions
4 leeks
200 ml oil
110 g olive oil
20 g goji berries
100 g goji infusion
salt

For the goji pearls

200 g isomalt
20 goji berries

For the base of the goji infusion

200 g water
2 g safflower
2 strands of saffron
1 g paprika
50 g goji berries
0.3 g xanthan gum

For the red goji puzzle

100 g infusion of goji
25 g ketchup
0.5 gellan gum
1.5 g agar agar

For the white goji puzzle

100 g cooked potato
25 g cream
75 g milk
30 g butter
1 g gellan gum
1.4 g agar agar
salt

method

For the paste

Grind all the ingredients to form a thick paste.

For the pigeon

Remove the pigeon breasts, season and add pinch of ginger and powdered liquorice. Smother with the paste and cook a la plancha. Set aside.
Use the carcases for the sauce.

For the pigeon sauce

Chop the carcases and brown them in a pan with a little oil.
Cut the vegetables and gently sauté separately with the remaining oil until lightly browned. Drain off the fat and add the vegetables to the carcases. Sauté well and cover with water. Reduce, strain and season. Add a few drops of oil at the last minute.
For each 150 g of pigeon sauce add 100 g of goji infusion and 50 g goji oil (this oil is obtained by crushing 100 g olive oil with 20 g goji berries).

For the goji pearls

Insert the tip of fine needles into each goji berry, one by one. Insert them into the isomalt which has previously been heated to melt it.
Leave to cool, withdraw the needles and store the berries in an airtight moisture-free container, until used.

For the base of the goji infusion

Boil the water and, off the heat, add the safflower, saffron, paprika and goji berries. Cover and leave to infuse for 5 minutes. Strain and add the xanthan gum. Blend and leave to rest.

For the red goji puzzle

Mix all ingredients and bring to boil for about 5 minutes. Leave the mixture to thicken and cut in the thermocut, creating figures similar to those shown in the picture.

For the white goji puzzle

Repeat the same process as in the previous step.

Place the pigeon sauce and pigeon breast on a plate. Arrange the red and white puzzles beside it. Spread the goji pearls between these pieces. Lightly season the pigeon.

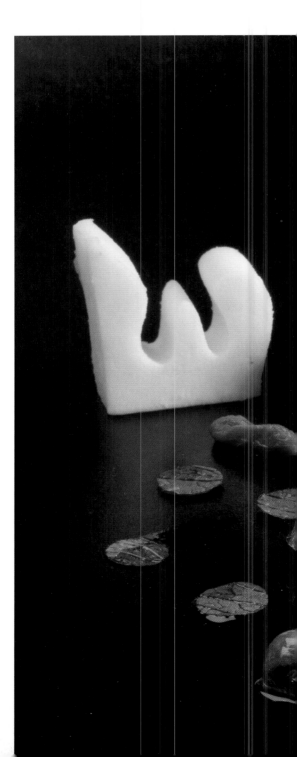

Pigeon with goji puzzle

The garden

Herbs are plants that once arose spontaneously in the field. Today they are cultivated in gardens for their aromatic qualities as condiments and even for their medicinal values. The leaves (sometimes also the stems and flowers) are usually used, whether fresh, dried, or dehydrated, both for seasoning stews and to enhance the aroma of culinary dishes, both raw and cooked. They are usually added – especially in the newest, most up-to-date cookery – at the last moment of cooking or when serving a dish, so that their greatest quality, which is of course their scent, remains unchanged. For a long time, herbs were mostly ignored, except mint and peppermint, as well as parsley – essential, above all in Basque cuisine. It is very curious

how mint and peppermint have been associated with desserts (especially those with chocolate) or soft drinks like mojito, but there are very traditional savoury recipes, such as Madrid stew and other savoury broths, where the help of peppermint is important, especially to degrease and flavour an overwhelming dish. Also mint is used with lamb in classical English cuisine, and closer to home, in the well-known recipe for Catalan broad beans.

But we are going to focus on the herbs in the recipes included here, such as chervil, dill and parsley.

Chervil is always recommended to be used alone for, when with other powerfully scented herbs such as basil, thyme and oregano, it loses its aroma and is overpowered by these. But it is perfectly matched with dill, also aniseed, or parsley or chives, which are not so fragrant. Chervil, along with chives, parsley and tarragon, forms part of the mixture or bouquet of fine herbs traditionally used in French cuisine.

On the other hand, dill is an herbaceous annual plant. It has been mentioned since ancient times... To my way of thinking, it holds a special place in cookery because its delicious flavour is not matched by any other herb. It goes well with all other fresh herbs, although, as it has a very marked flavour, it should be used in moderation in order not to swamp other herbs.

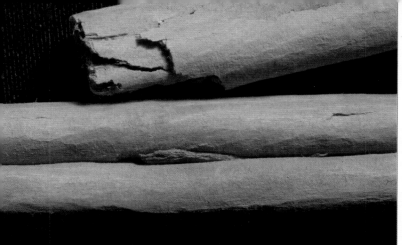

# of aromas

It is widely used in Scandinavian cuisine, is a very important ingredient in marinated salmon, and is used in canned herring and as a condiment in preserving gherkins and pickled cabbage. When used to flavour stews, soups, vegetables or hotpots, it should be added at the last moment, because cooking would destroy its decidedly aniseed aroma and flavour.

Finally, our soulmate: parsley is one of the most popular and well-known herbs in world cuisine and, without doubt, the most representative emblem of Basque cuisine. Above all, it is a basic component in the legendary recipe for green sauce, salsa verde! Anyway, the reason for its inclusion in these notes, despite being such an everyday – although never vulgar – herb, is due to its use in sweet recipes, which is really quite unique and very special.

Roasted peach with floral cotton

ingredients

4 people

For the roasted peach

2 peaches
1 vanilla pod
1 coffee teaspoon powdered sheep's milk
1 coffee teaspoon tomato powder
30 g sugar

For the oily sponge cake

90 g butter
160 g white chocolate
2 eggs
40 g sugar
50 g flour
1 g baking powder
1 tablespoon olive oil
sweet paprika

For the dried apricot purée

250 g water
50 g sugar
75 g dried apricots

For the cotton flowers

20 g sugar
pansies
freeze-dried parsley
sweet paprika

In addition

freeze-dried powdered parsley
powdered dried orange peel
sautéed diced peach

method

For the roasted peach

Peel and stone the peaches and cut them in perfect halves.
Halve the vanilla and rub the peaches with the vanilla, sugar, tomato and sheep's milk. Place in an oven dish and cover with a sheet of aluminium foil. Bake in the oven at 180°C for 20 minutes. Remove the sheet of aluminium and continue cooking for another 10 minutes.

For the oily sponge cake

Meanwhile, melt the butter and chocolate. Once melted, mix with the eggs, which have been beaten with the sugar. Finally, add the flour mixed with the baking powder.
Pour into a mould and bake at 180°C for 20 minutes. Turn out and leave to cool. Cut the sponge cake into small dice, lightly sauté in the oil and sprinkle with sweet paprika. Set aside.

For the dried apricot purée

Boil the water with the sugar and cook the dried apricots for 30 minutes over low heat. Purée and set aside in the fridge.

For the cotton flowers

Pour the sugar into a machine to make candy floss until the threads appear. Pick them up and form a ball. Place it between two sheets of parchment paper with some pansies, sweet paprika and freeze-dried parsley, and flatten it. Cut the sheets into 4 circles. Store in a dry place until ready to use.

Place the peaches on a plate and fill the hollow with the sautéed cake. Distribute around the purée of dried apricot and the diced peach. Sprinkle over the freeze-dried parsley powder and orange peel. At the last moment, place the flattened cotton on the surface.

Volcano of aromas

4 people

For inside the bag

80 g fresh garlic
8 mangosteen slices (*Garcinia mangostana*)
4 garlic cloves (cooked in milk for 9 minutes)
chervil leaves
dill
25 g virgin olive oil
8 crayfish tails (dipped in the sauce)
salt
pepper
ground ginger

For the crayfish sauce

50 g toasted bread
15 g chorizo pulp
75 g toasted almonds
20 g oil
1 ripe tomato
1 tablespoon sherry vinegar
salt
sugar

For the cinnamon aroma

1 cinnamon stick

In addition

8 crayfish heads

method

For inside the bag

Mix all ingredients gently and place in a container. Set aside.

For the crayfish sauce

Crush all the ingredients together. Season.

For the cinnamon aroma

For this operation, you need the device called a Volcano. Insert the cinnamon stick, in small pieces, into the part of the machine where you place the product whose aroma you wish to extract. Place all the ingredients stored in the container into the bag and close it, attach it to the machine and let it run for 2 minutes. The bag will inflate with the flavoured air that will be extracted. After this time, place it in the oven at 220°C for 4 minutes.

Serve the bag closed, and open it in front of the diners to appreciate the aromas.
Accompany the dish with the crayfish heads opened lengthwise and toasted in a pan with a little sauce.

What a pair

As
long ago as the
18th century, a cookery
treatise said some very far-sighted
things about eggs: 'They divide
themselves between the healthy and the sick,
the poor and the rich.' Besides being a soft and
agreeable food, like few others, eggs are the height
of versatility, as they go with everything, precisely
because of their aromatic neutrality and smoothness.
One of the most amusing travel books ever (*Gathering
from Spain*), written by Richard Ford and published at
the end of the 19th century, refers to Hispanic cookery,
saying: 'fried eggs are at all times the most humble culinary
resource'.

But eggs in their various forms have not always been
associated with purely rural, simple, or home cooking. In
the recipes of Aragonese Teodoro Bardají (the so-called
Hispanic Escoffier) there are innumerable recipes using
eggs, which, excluding tortillas, number exactly forty-
nine recipes! Some as curious as Eggs a la Bella Otero,
The Rainbow, The Muscovite, or Eggs Fru-Fru,
some served cold and with various jellies. This
culinary author has been more sparing in his
use of eggs as a main ingredient, but no
less brilliant.

I
have always given
great importance to eggs in
my cooking. And there is always a
dish representing this on our menu. But
I have worried constantly about poached eggs
because – despite it being a marvel of smoothness
not to break the runny yolks – dropping them in
water with vinegar and salt, loses much of their property
and flavour. So a few years ago, we developed a simple
plastic device, where you could introduce the whole egg
with aromatic and fatty additions, in this case black truffle
and 'tartufo' oil, in such a way that you could poach the egg
without it coming into contact with water. It is the base of a
dish that has been successful for many years, 'Egg and Truffle
Flower in Goose Fat with Txistorra of Dates'. Take some
bread and... dunk it in. The magnificence of simplicity.
So perhaps you don't need to wrack your brains about
eggs but just follow the wise advice of the Andalusian
proverb: 'Eat an egg one hour old, bread of the same
day, wine a year old and chicken a little less than
a year.' And, apart from the wine, I fully agree
with these words.

Graffiti of elliptical egg

ingredients

4 people

For the eggs

4 eggs (60 g each)

For the garlic and pepper cake

3 garlic cloves
2 eggs
40 g isomalt
1 piquillo pepper
60 g flour
100 ml olive oil 0.4 °

For the green powder

20 g spinach
15 g parsley, without leaves
15 g chives

For the green lacquer

1 bunch of parsley
2 drops white truffle oil

For the black lacquer

1 squid (300 g)
squid ink consommé
1 onion
2 green peppers
1 garlic clove
1 small tomato
4 tablespoons olive oil
½ glass red wine
2.5 litres water
salt
powdered sarsaparilla

For the clarified squid sauce broth

1 squid (300 g)
the remaining black lacquer broth
1 carrot
1 spring onion
1 leek
5 egg whites
1 g lovage (*Levisticum officinale*)
salt

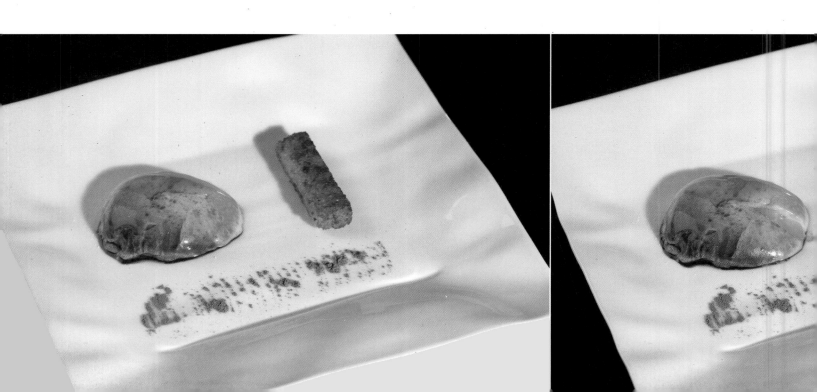

method

For the eggs

Cook the eggs whole in their shells in salt water at 75.2°C for 12 minutes. Leave to stand 1 minute. Break the shell carefully and place the egg on a plate.

For the garlic and pepper cake

Boil two cloves of garlic. Once boiled, chop them to form a paste. Slice the remaining garlic and fry it in olive oil. Then chop it finely. Reserve the boiled and fried garlic separately.
Beat the eggs together with the isomalt until they rise up. Once beaten, add the garlic (fried and boiled) and the pepper, cut into brunoise. Add the flour gently, without eroding the emulsion. Bake in a cake mould at 180°C for 16 minutes. Once cold, cut the cake into 10 x 2 cm sticks and fry them in olive oil. Drain them well.

For the green powder

Place all the herbs in a container and dehydrate them at 50°C. Then pulverize them together.

For the green lacquer

Blend only the parsley leaves and strain through a fine sieve. Add the truffle oil.

For the black lacquer

Cut the onion, peppers and garlic into julienne strips and fry in the oil. Clean the squid and separate the ink. Chop all the meat into not too small pieces.
When the vegetables have been sautéed, add the squid meat and sauté it all together. Add the tomato cut into pieces and cook until it just dissolves. Moisten with wine and leave to reduce. Add the inks, diluted with water. Stir and cover with water.
Leave to cook for 30 minutes over medium heat. Separate all the meat and crush the rest. Strain twice, ending with a cheesecloth but returning to the heat to be warmed after each straining.
Season and add a pinch of sarsaparilla.
Fill the spray with the black broth to lacquer the egg, reserving the rest.

For the clarified squid sauce broth

Clean the squid and reserve the ink for the black lacquer.
Chop the squid into brunoise and add to the vegetables, which have also been cut into brunoise, and incorporate the egg whites, forming a mass; leave to rest for 45 minutes in the refrigerator.
Bring the broth that remains from the previous step to the boil and add the mass prepared with the egg whites and vegetables. When it comes to the boil, shock the pan with some ice. Leave to simmer. Strain through a fine sieve. Infuse with the lovage. Season.

Using a spray, lacquer the egg black and green.
Arrange the egg to the left of the plate, placing the cake parallel to it.
In front of both draw a line with powder.
In front of each diner, make an incision, breaking the egg, and spread the clarified broth over the emerging yolk.

From the egg to the chicken

ingredients

4 people

For the juice and chicken broth

1 cleaned chicken (800 g)
1.2 g xanthan gum (for every 500 ml broth)
1 tablespoon olive oil 0,4°
2.5 litres water
salt
freeze-dried chicken (reduced to powder)
pepper

For the eggs

4 eggs (60 g each)
freeze-dried chicken (reduced to powder)
freeze-dried yolk (reduced to powder)
salt

For the lacquered skin

the skins of 2 chickens
50 g isomalt sugar
50 g glucose
100 g fondant

For the yolk veil

50 g freeze-dried egg powder
50 g agar agar
25 g icing sugar
dash of olive oil

In addition

2 tablespoons balsamic vinegar reduction

method

For the juice and chicken broth

Place the chicken on a baking sheet, lightly seasoned with oil and roast for one hour at 190°C. Then collect all the juices from the roast and reduce by half. Strain and set aside.
Place the chicken in a pot and cover with water. Cook on low heat for 4 hours. Strain the broth and add body to its texture with xanthan gum. Season and add a pinch of freeze-dried chicken to the broth.

For the eggs

Bake the eggs whole, in the shell, in water for 8 minutes at 75.2°C. Leave to stand one minute. Break the shell carefully and place the egg on a plate. Season and add freeze-dried chicken and egg powder. Pour the egg carefully into a hot pan, to which has been added a tablespoon of fat from the roast. Sear on both sides and add more freeze-dried chicken powder. Set aside.

For the lacquered skin

Dry the chicken skins well with a cloth. Spread the skins on baking parchment. Cover with another sheet of paper and place a weight on top to prevent the skins from shrinking.
Mix the remaining ingredients in a saucepan and heat to 160°C. Allow to cool and reduce to powder.
Once the skins are dry, remove the paper and sprinkle the powdered sugar over them. Arrange them on a salamander-type heat source to caramelise. Leave to rest and cut into irregular shapes.

For the yolk veil

Mix the ingredients.
Grease a plastic mould, 20 x 10 cm, with some oil. Sprinkle with the powder and shake off the excess.
Boil the mould upside down in a steamer at 119°C for 15 seconds.
Lift from the steamer and remove the veil that will have formed, from the mould.

Serve the chicken broth in a soup bowl. Sprinkle the crispy skin vertically to form a solid line. On both sides of it add a drop of balsamic vinegar reduction and six drops of reduced chicken juice. Above the skin place the fried egg and, above it, a hint of crispy skin. Cover the whole with the yolk veil.

Smoke from hot coals

It's true to say that we have included in this commentary a number of varied recipes, that use smoke and its raison d'être, the purifying and blazing coals, as well as those with the undesirable effect of an overdose of heat i.e. burning with its unique and bitter aftertaste, which we have converted into something agreeable and very pleasant.

On the one hand, it is well-known that smoking is a conservation technique lost back in the mists of time. The mastery of fire brought about the protective evening bonfire, which became the centre of the home in cave dwellings. Thus, between the needs of the pantry and pure chance, this wise observation of our ancestors was born: within the cave, foods kept closest to the fire and touched by smoke kept the best. Since those far-off times, one can definitely speak of two different cultures of drying, arising from different living conditions and climates: the culture of the sun and that of smoking, the latter emerging in cold countries that lacked sunshine or in the forest areas of Africa where there was enough wood. In any case, this smoke produced not only a

slow drying and antiseptic purifying action on food, but also helped keep it fit for consumption, at the same time providing that which most interests us in cooking today, the delicate, unique and unmistakable aroma and flavour of smoked oak.

Following our 'most difficult yet' – it sounds like a circus but is very serious – experiments with smoked chocolate, which we discussed at great length, we have now focused on citrus fruits. In two ways, on the one hand with ice cream, in this case lemon with a smoky touch (producing a pungent combination of acidity from the fruit and the aroma and light taste of smoke) and on the other hand, transforming the citrus into a hot coal for fish – in this case, sole – giving it the taste of the grill and that touch of acidity.

Another but different issue is that of burning. This is not something new, and I dare say it is quite ancient. It is the case with scorched, curdled sheep's milk (mamia) where the pastors of the Navarre Valley of Baztan prepared it, it is known as *gaztanbera*, using a technique thousands of years old, absolutely authentic and artesanal. Using the milk of Latxa sheep and natural rennet, warming the milk through stones and requiring the use of a truncated wooden bowl of wood, called *kaiku*, it is a method, which clearly inspired our own Burnt Milk.

Cassia steam with citrus cake

ingredients

4 people

For the albumin orange cake

100 g egg yolks
50 g orange juice
3 coffee spoons egg whites
120 g icing sugar
50 g walnut powder
50 g almond powder
25 g flour
orange zest

For the apricot and cinnamon mousse

150 g apricot flesh
75 g water
15 g sugar
½ cinnamon stick
1 sheet gelatine

For the dried fruit muesli

20 g breadcrumbs
15 g hazelnut pieces
15 g sliced almonds
15 g peeled sliced walnuts
25 g melted butter
15 g isomalt sugar
4 g cornflour (corn starch)
15 g white wine
5 g millet
salt

For the cassia stock

400 g water
50 g sugar
½ cinnamon stick
15 g cassia bark (*Cinnamomum aromaticum*)
juice of one lemon

In addition

25 g solid carbon dioxide (dry ice)
1 green apple, cut into sticks
grated carob

method

For the albumin orange cake

Beat the egg yolks and set aside. Separately, mix the orange juice with the egg whites and icing sugar. When well beaten, mix with the egg yolks. Meanwhile, thoroughly mix the walnut, almond and flour and add to the mixture of egg whites and yolks. At the last moment, add the zest of an orange. Spread over a mould and bake at 180°C for 18 minutes. Once cooked, cut into rectangles, 5 x 1 cm. Set aside.

For the apricot and cinnamon mousse

Boil the mixture of apricot pulp, water, sugar and cinnamon stick for 8 minutes. Then add the gelatine soaked in cold water. Remove the cinnamon stick and insert the mixture into a syphon and charge it once. Leave to stand in the cold for 2 hours.

For the dried fruit muesli

Knead everything gently and form some cookies on a silicone sheet. Bake at 175°C until crispy. Once cool, cut into small pieces.

For the cassia stock

Cook all the ingredients, except the lemon juice, simmer 15 minutes. Strain, add lemon juice and reserve.

Place the apricot mousse in the centre of a soup bowl; on it, the strips of sponge cake and the grated carob. On this place the apple sticks, in such a way that it has the same volume as the cake. Sprinkle the muesli on the surface in a haphazard way. Arrange the carbon dioxide (dry ice) around this and, in front of the diners, pour over the hot cassia broth, causing a cloud of smoke.

Smoked lemon
ice cream

ingredients

4 people

1 litre milk
1 vanilla pod
300 g lemon curd
100 g lemon juice
5 egg yolks

method

Boil the milk with the vanilla pod for 1
minute. Mix the lemon juice with lemon
curd and smoke for 15 minutes in a smoker.
Off the heat, add the egg yolks to the milk
and mix well, as if for a crème anglaise. Heat
up to 70°C. Open the vanilla, take all the
seeds out and add them to the cream. Mix
all ingredients and blend thoroughly.

Place the mixture in an ice-cream
maker, and when ready serve at
a suitable temperature (from -3
to -5°C)

Sole with barbecued citrus

ingredients

4 people

For the sole

1 sole, 800 g
olive oil 0.4 °
salt
ground ginger

For the sole mojo

50 g hazelnut butter
30 g lettuce leaves (coloured on la plancha)
10 g dried squid
15 g cooked white beans
1 tablespoon sherry vinegar
20 g meat stock
salt
pepper

For lateral bones of the sole

the sole bones
100 ml olive oil 0.4 °
salt

For the sole sauce

500 g beef consommé
2 g xanthan gum
1 g lemon grass
1 onion, gently sautéed
salt
white pepper

For the barbecued orange and lemon

1 orange
1 lemon

In addition

balsamic vinegar
shiso shoots

method

For the sole

Clean the sole and fillet it, removing the four fillets. Set aside the sole bones.
Fold each fillet back on itself, forming a ring and secure with a toothpick.
Season and add the ginger. Set aside.

For the sole mojo

Crush the ingredients. Season and set aside.

For lateral bones of the sole

Fry the bones in oil until crisp. Season.

For the sole sauce

Dilute the gum in the consommé. Boil the ingredients over low heat for 5 minutes. Strain the sauce and season.

For the barbecued orange and lemon

Grill the orange and lemon until they turn a beautiful golden hue.

Spread the sole with the mojo and brown it on both sides in a pan with a little oil, keeping it juicy.
Remove the toothpicks.
Pour the sauce into a shallow dish; arrange the sole and its fringe of fried bones.
Garnish with a slice of orange and a slice of lemon.
Decorate the plate with a few drops of balsamic vinegar and shiso.

Shrimps and pandanus

ingredients

4 people

For the shrimp

12 large shrimp (*crangon crangon*)
oak and sandalwood sawdust
200 g red wine salt (300 g red wine
   and 200 g coarse salt)

For the pandanus broth

400 g water
20 g sugar
the green part of half a leek
2 pandanus slices (*Pandanus hornei*)
salt
pepper

For the leek sheet

4 green leaves of leek
200 g pandanus broth
salt
pepper

For the red wine salt

100 g red wine
40 g salt

In addition

mint leaves

method

For the shrimp

Place the shrimp in the salt for 15 minutes.
Clean away the salt and lightly wash. Dry
and smoke them for 15 minutes in the
sawdust of oak mixed with sandalwood. Set
aside.

For the pandanus broth

Cook all ingredients except the pandanus
for half an hour over low heat. Off the heat,
add the pandanus and leave for 15 minutes.
Strain and add a pinch of salt and pepper.

For the leek sheet

Vacuum-pack the ingredients and cook at
70°C for 90 minutes. Set aside.

For the red wine salt

Cold mix both ingredients. Spread the
mixture on a tray and leave to dry at room
temperature. Set aside.

Place the hot leek sheet at the bottom of the dish. Over it, the freshly smoked
shrimps. All around a little wine salt and a few mint leaves. Cover everything
with a chafing dish so that it arrives at the table with the delicate aromas of
smoke and pandanus. Serve the pandanus broth separately in a jug.

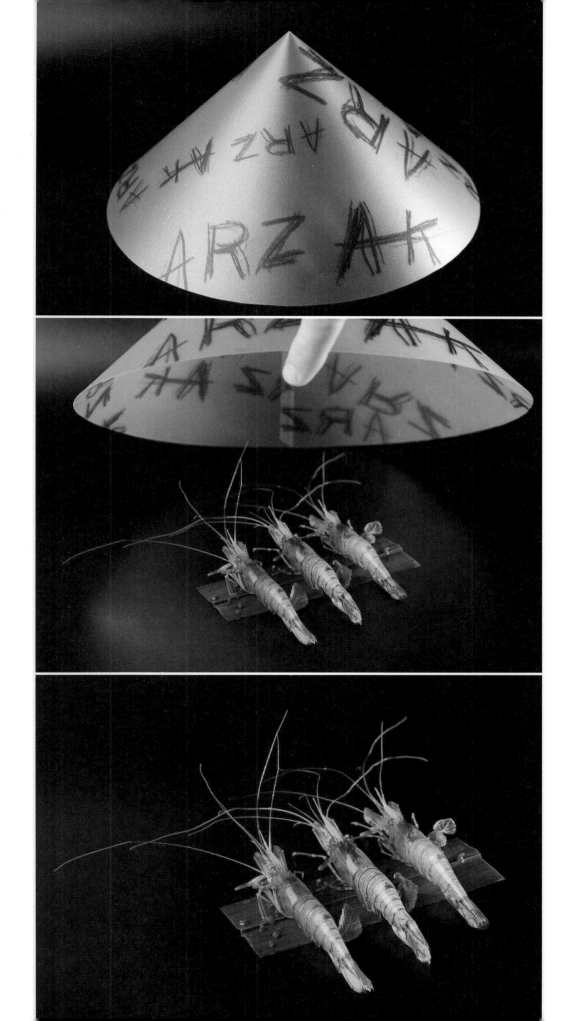

An agreeable

Talk of syringes will seem creepy to many, having nothing to do with gastronomy but linked with medicine. But do not panic, for the use of this tool in the kitchen isn't at all aggressive or painful, but culinarily pleasurable.

The idea of using the syringe came to me some time ago when I saw a very modern slice of French toast being prepared in the kitchen and served in the restaurant.

Something that no one can deny is that the most fundamental virtue of good French toast – whether called toast, *pan perdu*, French Toast to the Americans, or Poor Knights of Windsor to the English – is that it must be completely soaked to make it juicy and prevent it from being hard as a brick. The most common way of preparing it is to soak the bread or brioche in flavoured milk, light custard, or wine (according to tradition). In our case, the atypical French toast, which I referred to above, was rye bread with melon sauce, to which had also been added raspberry brandy, peach liquor, cream, etc., to soak it perfectly. But using the syringe, we leapt forward with this recipe, injecting a syringe of hot melon sauce into the slice of brioche (fried and caramelised), submerging it within seconds in melon sauce. In this way the liquid penetrated inside almost instantly.

On the other hand, the syringe has been used in cookery for a long time with certain types of meat, such as chicken and other birds, adding flavour and juiciness using certain wines or spirits.

It seems to me the syringe has a perfect use in home cooking for injecting liquids into cakes or muffins. It is the ideal tool for making 'drunken' bizcochitos without spilling a drop. For example, if you want muffins with a chocolate filling, a sleeve works well, but if the filling is more fluid the task becomes very complicated and it is best to use a syringe.

In our new recipes, we give flavour injections to crayfish with corn and almond mash, as well as lamb penetrated with stout.

and tasty jab

Crayfish injected with corn

ingredients

4 people

For the crayfish

8 crayfish (90 g each)

For the crayfish injection

100 g corn
10 g almond paste
salt
ginger
liquorice

For the corn vinaigrette

100 g corn oil
12 g sherry vinegar
26 g truffle juice
2 g salt
60 g corn

In addition

fried rice noodles
olive oil

method

For the crayfish

Remove the pincers from the crayfish and reserve for other uses.
Cut the body of the crayfish lengthwise in half with a slicing machine.

For the crayfish injection

Mix all the ingredients. Crush them and strain them.
Put the open crayfish in the corn mixture so that they are completely covered.
Repeatedly puncture the flesh of the crustaceans with 5 syringes (with very fine needles) joined together. Leave to stand at least 10 minutes. Set aside.

For the corn vinaigrette

Mix all ingredients, except the corn. Add the corn that has been taken from the cob.

Cook the crayfish a la plancha with a dash of oil, keeping them juicy. Place the crayfish on the plate so that they recover their original shape; place a fried rice noodle, split into three pieces, on each crayfish at the open part of the tail. On one side, drizzle the preparation for the injection, heated with a pinch of corn oil and, over this, the vinaigrette.

Malt beer injected lamb

ingredients

4 people

For the lamb injection

1 litre water
100 ml dark beer
1 bunch of parsley
4 garlic cloves
10 g soy sauce
3 g powdered ginger
1 g liquorice powder
salt
pepper

For the lamb

800 g rack of lamb (200 g per serving)

For the freeze-dried beer

1 bottle (33 cl) dark beer
25 g sugar
25 g albumin (powdered egg white)

For the beer stock

500 g lamb bones
2 onions
1 garlic clove
1 shallot
250 ml water
250 ml lamb stock
20 g dark beer
3 g powdered hop
salt
pepper

For the strands of tatsoi

80 g tatsoi leaves (*Brassica narinosa*)
20 g olive oil 0.4 °
2.5 g rice vinegar
salt
pepper

For the beer gelatine

½ bottle lager (33 cl)
16 g gelatine

method

For the lamb injection

Cook all the ingredients for 15 minutes. Strain through cheesecloth. Put the broth in the injection machine.

For the lamb

Inject the above broth into the lamb and leave to stand for at least 24 hours.
After this time, thoroughly clean the lamb and cut into portions.
Brown well on both sides, keeping it juicy. Set aside.

For the freeze-dried beer

Beat the mix of beer, sugar and albumin vigorously, as if for a meringue. When well risen, place a few irregular spoonfuls on a tray and put it in the freezer. Once frozen, put the beer preparation in the freeze-dryer at a temperature of -50.5°C and 0.065 mb pressure. It will take approximately 24 hours to freeze-dry. Set aside in a dry vacuum.

For the beer stock

Colour the bones slightly with a dash of oil. Add the garlic, onions and shallots cut in julienne and sauté for a few minutes. Deglaze and moisten with stock and water. Simmer for 2 hours. Strain.
At the last moment, add 20 g of dark beer and 3 g of powdered hop per 100 g of sauce. Add salt and pepper. Set aside.

For the strands of tatsoi

Cut the leaves in a triangular shape, keeping the stem, and season with the mixture of the other ingredients.

For the beer gelatine

Hydrate the gelatine leaf and incorporate it into the beer that has been boiled. Leave to cool. When it hardens, lightly chop it with a knife. Set aside.

Place the lamb on a plate with
the freeze-dried beer beside it.
Accompany it with a small salad of
beer gelatine and tatsoi.
Serve with the sauce in a separate jug
and pour the very hot sauce over the
freeze-dried beer to melt it.

Sweet, healthy and natural

I have no doubt that isomalt is a new term that sounds strange at the moment, but within no time will be incorporated into our everyday vocabulary.

It's a new sugar substitute that is curiously derived exclusively from sugar, has the same taste profile, as well as the same appearance, but only half the calories of sugar, is suitable for diabetics, and is not hygroscopic, i.e. it doesn't stick.

This substitute is not artificial since it is produced exclusively from sugar beet and therefore its sweetness is pure, without any strange aftertaste.

In its manufacture, first the sugar fructose and glucose are combined, again with the help of natural enzymes, and in the second stage hydrogenation takes place. The result is a new substance, comparable to sugar in many respects. It has the same profile as sugar, the same appearance and works virtually the same – even better – than sugar.

Its nutritional value is approximately 2 calories per gram, or just half that of sugar. Aware of the delicate metabolism of diabetics, it perfectly meets their energy needs. Serious scientific studies show that, after ingestion of isomalt, the increase of glucose and insulin in the blood is very small. For this reason diabetics can consume products sweetened with isomalt without any problem.

In the same way, it is very important for children, and something that is of great concern to parents, it does not cause tooth decay. As the microorganisms of the mouth cannot use isomalt so the plaque acids that can dissolve tooth enamel are not formed.

There are many products today that include isomalt in their preparation, sweets, chewing gum, chocolates and baked goods, among others. It is estimated that more than a thousand products already contain it.

In confectionery, it is ideal for making sweets, offering high resistance to moisture thus making them much more durable; they are not sticky nor do they go soft at high temperatures or in very humid areas. Furthermore, they present themselves in a pretty, totally transparent, crystal colour.

'Lacasitos' inverted

ingredients

4 people

For the inside

200 g isomalt

For the outside

200 g chocolate

In addition

Cocoa powder

method

For the inside

Melt the isomalt, heating it up to 160°C. Spread it between two silpats, forming a thin layer. Leave to harden and cut into small pieces.

For the outside

Chop the chocolate and melt it.
Bathe the isomalt pieces in chocolate to form a thin layer around the crisp sheet. Set aside.

Sprinkle each piece of chocolate with lots of cocoa powder and store in a container for presentation.

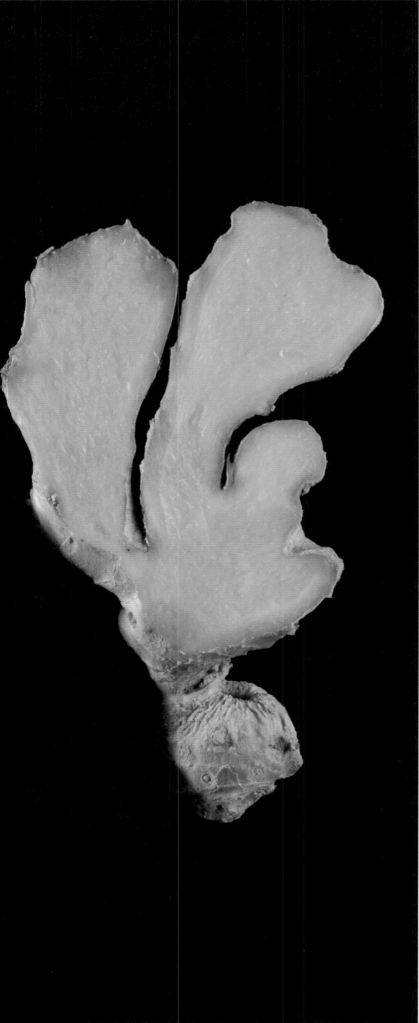

Cultural

It's only too well-known that the innovative movements of the Seventies, which began in France and took root elsewhere, brought about a complete revolution of many traditional concepts, the most noteworthy being the rejection of all useless complication and the discovery of the aesthetics of simplicity, which together with other principles, such as reducing cooking times and a daring mix of new tastes, meant that Western cuisine logically began to look, even if only out of the corner of one eye, to Eastern cultures, where this type of cooking had been practiced in many ways since time immemorial.

Today this all sounds like ancient history because, in fact, miscegenation, fusion and oriental cooking influences – Chinese, Japanese or Thai and others – are now tangible. Not only through their specific restaurants, proliferating throughout our country, but also because they influence all of the most creative cuisine, both in the products used – given the globalisation of the marketplace – as well as in the techniques and the thousand and one details extracted from the Far, but increasingly near, East, to the point that the exotic is slowly turning into the everyday and becoming part of our culinary habits.

One of the products that best represents this bridge between East and West is undoubtedly ginger i.e. the thick root, underground rhizome of the attractive flowering plant (*Zingiber officinale*). It is used intensively and widely in Asian cookery, where only salt is given more importance. It has been cultivated in tropical Asia from more than 3,000 years, although its exact origin is unknown.

bridge

Ginger was also used in the Middle East and in southern Europe well before the Roman era. The Portuguese introduced it to Africa, the Spanish took it to the West Indies and, by the 16th century, Spain had a flourishing trade in Jamaican ginger with the rest of Europe.

With a clean, fresh and spicy flavour, ginger goes well in many dishes, both sweet and savoury, although where it makes the most of its potential is in the East.

It comes in many forms: fresh, dried, pickled, preserved in syrup, and crystallised. Chinese cuisine prefers to use it fresh rather than dried, both for its flavour and texture. Chopped, crushed or cut into sticks, it is used to season many meat, fish and vegetable dishes.

Pink pickled ginger, called gari in Japan, is the usual seasoning for sushi. The Japanese even have a special tool, the oroshigane, which is used to grate fresh ginger.

Try to keep a little fresh ginger in the kitchen in the fridge, as well as an especially fine grater. Grated ginger and its juice dramatically enhance any dish, but must always be served with restraint.

Ginger is crucial in preparing curries, with soy sauce, in stewed meat and poultry, in chutneys, vegetable soups, in fish dishes and cheese dishes, in stewed and baked fruits, in pies, tarts, cookies, cakes, sweet breads, in spiced beverages and wines.

the gelatine revival

The sway of fashion significantly affects
gastronomy and cooking. Today, when merely
talking about omnipresent gelatines, it is good
to know the history of the more baroque and
grandiloquent version, which has come to be
called aspic. Once-fashionable things later
disappear and, after many years, sometimes
centuries, again rise charmingly to the fore.
This is what happened with gelatines.
Aspics have been used all through
the ages: in the culinary art of the
Greeks and Romans, the famous
and only aspic was the eel. And now gelatines
and gelées are back on the crest of a wave, with
all those preparations like cold gelatinized soups,
beautiful little goblets, showing the complexity
of preparation and ingredients in superimposed
congealed layers.

The price we had to pay before, the constant
gumminess, has now thankfully been replaced by
immediacy and subtlety.

The term aspic also has a logical explanation.
The name comes from the mottled, cold, icy-
looking preparation, reminiscent of the skin and
characteristics of the asp snake.

Increasingly, we are discovering more types of
gelatine. Currently one of the most interesting gels
is kappa.

Kappa is extracted from a type of red algae (from the
genera *Chondrus* and *Eucheuma*). It is a carrageenan,
a name derived from the Irish town of Carragheen,
where they have used these algae for over 600 years. In
the mid-twentieth century, this 'Irish moss' started to
be produced industrially as a gel. Kappa provides a gel
with a firm, brittle texture.

This gelatine comes in fine powder and, unlike other
gelatines, is mixed cold and then brought to the boil. Its
rapid gelling allows quick thickening of a product, and
once gelled, it can withstand temperatures up to 60°C. In
acidic media it loses some of its gelling capacity. One of
its most interesting aspects is its texture, for this gelatine is
firm and brittle.

A bundle of lobster and flowers

ingredients

For the beta-carotene juice

250 g carrot juice
50 g olive oil
5 g sherry vinegar
10 g truffle juice
3 g soy sauce
25 g tomato liquid
salt

For the sautéed lobster

2 lobsters (350 g each)
1 clove garlic, chopped
pinch of chopped parsley
20 g virgin olive oil
salt
ground ginger
ground liquorice

For the salad and its dressing

50 g peanut oil
8 g sherry vinegar
15 g truffle juice
3 g sesame oil
red chard, tatsoi, arugula sprouts, mustard
  sprouts, shiso sprouts and purple shiso
  sprouts
salt
black pepper

For the beta-carotene sheet

200 g carrot juice
3 g kappa

For the kohlrabi sheet

100 g kohlrabi juice
1.5 g kappa

In addition

fennel leaves
chervil
crunchy corn

method

For the beta-carotene juice

Reduce the carrot juice to 100 g. Leave to cool. Cold mix the ingredients, season and reserve.

For the sautéed lobster

Split the lobsters in half and separate the tails and pinchers (reserve the heads for other uses).
Season the tails and sauté them with oil, garlic and a pinch of chopped parsley. Lightly scald the pinchers in boiling water. Remove the meat and repeat the same operation with the tails. Add a pinch of salt, ginger and liquorice to the whole.

For the salad and its dressing

To prepare the vinaigrette, cold mix the peanut oil, sesame oil, vinegar, truffle juice, salt and pepper.
At the last minute, dress a piece of each vegetable that will be in the salad.

For the beta-carotene sheet

Cold mix both ingredients and boil them. Spread very thinly onto a plastic plate. Once gelled, cut in sheets, 12 x 12 cm. Store on parchment paper until ready to use.

For the kohlrabi sheet

Repeat the same preparation as above with the kohlrabi and cut it into rectangular sheets of 2 x10 cm. Set aside.

Once the lobster has been sautéed, place it in the beta-carotene juice for 5 seconds.
Arrange the salad and the lobster in alternate layers on a flat dish, giving some volume to the arrangement. Add a few crunchy corn as well. Surround everything with the sheet of beta-carotene.
At the side arrange a row of chervil and fennel leaves interspersed, and cover them with the transparent kohlrabi sheet.

igers

ingredients

4 people

For the mussels

12 large mussels
20 g olive oil

For the tomato layer

250 g tomato sauce
10 g kappa

For the tomato sauce

1 onion
3 very ripe large tomatoes
30 g Worcester sauce
salt
pepper
ground ginger
2 tablespoons virgin olive oil

For the green escabeche

300 g spinach
400 g water
25 g sugar
1 garlic clove
1 medium onion, in julienne
zest of half an orange
75 g rice vinegar
150 g olive oil
50 g water from the cooked mussels

For the black oil

20 g black sesame seeds
20 g extra virgin olive oil
salt

method

For the mussels

Pour the mussels into a pan with the oil and leave for a couple of minutes to open. Remove the shells and freeze for 24 hours. Reserve the cooking juices.

For the tomato layer

Cold mix both ingredients and bring to the boil. When at 60°C, dip in the frozen mussels using a needle. Leave at room temperature for one hour. Set aside.

For the tomato sauce

Brown the onion in the oil. Add the remaining ingredients and leave on a low flame for 30 minutes. Crush and strain.

For the green escabeche

Boil the spinach with the water and sugar for 3 minutes. Purée, strain and reserve.
Separately, fry the onion and garlic in oil. Add the orange zest, vinegar and reserved cooking juices. Simmer 30 minutes over low heat. Add the spinach and shred everything in the Thermomix. Strain. Set aside.

For the black oil

Cold mix both ingredients and strain. Add salt and set aside.

Place the green escabeche in a spoon shaped like a mussel shell; place a mussel dipped in tomato sauce on top and finally add a few spots of black oil. Serve at room temperature and eat as a snack.

If you are lucky enough to have a mould magnetized at the bottom like the one in the photo, you can present this in ways that defy the laws of physics.

Oysters with red pepper

ingredients

4 people

For the oysters

12 oysters
200 ml olive oil 0.4 °
ground ginger
liquid nitrogen

For the outer layer of the oyster

180 g red piquillo peppers
1 clove garlic, minced
2 tablespoons olive oil
5 g angelica
150 g water
5 g kappa (per 100 g of preparation)
salt
sugar

For the oyster sauce

4 tablespoons olive oil
1 onion
1 green pepper
50 g potato
2 juniper berries
1 g aniseed grains
4 oysters
10 g nori
250 g vegetable broth
pinch of safflower
salt

For the green leek 'silk'

the green of 3 leeks
salt

In addition

violet flowers
Sichuan shoots (*Zanthoxylum piperitum*)

method

For the oysters

Open the oysters and remove them from the shell. Cut off the outer beards and sprinkle with ginger. Freeze in liquid nitrogen, leaving flat.
Fry the oyster beards in hot oil.

For the outer layer of the oyster

Sauté the garlic in oil in a saucepan. As soon as it colours, add the red peppers (without seeds) and sauté everything. Moisten with water and add the angelica. Cook for 5 minutes, crush and strain. Season and add a pinch of sugar.
Per 100 g of prepared piquillo peppers add 5 g of kappa. Crush the peppers with the gelatine and bring to the boil.
Dip in the oysters, creating a red cape around them. Set aside.

For the oyster sauce

Chop the onion and green pepper and sauté gently with oil. When half cooked, add the chopped potatoes, juniper berries and aniseed and sauté everything. Add the oysters and nori seaweed and continue sautéing. Moisten with the broth and cook another 5 minutes. Purée and strain. If too thick, add water or oyster juice to thin down. Finally, add a pinch of safflower. Add salt to taste.

For the green leek 'silk'

Chop the leeks and cook them in salted water for 3 minutes. Keep back a little cooking water. Crush the leeks with a little cooking water leaving a fibrous mixture which will be spread over a silicone sheet and left to dry.
Once dry, cut it into pieces.

Place three red oysters in a shallow dish. Spread the sauce parallel to them and on it place the fried oyster beards, the leek 'silk', Sichuan sprouts and flower petals.

Kefir, sometimes known as Bulgarian yogurt and in Chile, as birds' yogurt, is the oldest fermented milk that exists. Its origin lies in the mountains of the Caucasus. It has special and valuable properties, as evidenced by the longevity of the people who have consumed it regularly for thousands of years.

Caucasian Muslims believed that the kefir ferment (or grains of the Prophet Mohammed) would lose their strength if people of other religions used them. Therefore, preparation of kefir has long been kept secret. It is believed that the word kefir comes from *keif*, a Turkish word which means pleasant sensation.

In the past, it was hardly known outside the Caucasus, although Marco Polo mentions it in the stories of his travels to the East. It was almost forgotten for five centuries until, at the beginning of the 19th century, when it was used therapeutically against tuberculosis in European sanatoria. The longevity of the people, who traditionally consumed it, has popularised it in Europe since the beginning of the 20th century.

eternal youth

Kefir is a fungus, a mixture of bacteria and yeasts, which live in symbiosis. There are three types: milk kefir, water kefir and kefir of tea or kombucha.

This creamy beverage, similar to yogurt, has several distinctive features: 7 bacteria are involved in its fermentation, compared to 3 or 4 in yogurt, and the whey, wherein reside its most beneficial elements, are not removed. It is completely digestible, regulates the digestive system and restores intestinal flora.

It's like a kind of yogurt. The flavour will depend on how long the milk is left in the fungus. It's usually left for 24 hours and any time thereafter will make it more sour in taste. Despite its many virtues, kefir is too unstable to be produced commercially, so it is difficult to find on supermarket shelves. Since at the moment its preparation is completely by hand, here are some points to consider before making it at home. If you are going to be away for a few days and cannot take it with you, leave it in sugar and water in the fridge for 3 or 4 days, and if you are going to be away for longer than that, drain it thoroughly, dry it and freeze it, because then it will last for several months.

apple kefir and atomised fruits

ingredients

4 people

For the caramelised apple rings

1 apple (Basque variety Errezila)

For the kefir and foie filling

200 g fresh foie gras
55 g cream cheese
45 g kefir
1 tablespoon virgin olive oil
salt
black pepper
powdered ginger
liquorice powder

For the atomised fruits

2 raspberries
2 blackberries
grapefruit segments, membrane removed
orange segments, membrane removed
liquid nitrogen

In addition

chopped chives
sugar
virgin olive oil

method

For the caramelised apple rings

Peel and slice the apple horizontally into slices 1.5 cm thick. Remove the apple core with a round pastry cutter to get a hole 2 cm in diameter. Bake the rings at 175°C for 2 minutes. Set aside.

For the kefir and foie filling

Dice the foie gras and sauté it. Leave to stand for 5 minutes and crush it with the cream cheese, kefir, and oil. Season with salt and pepper and add a pinch of ginger and liquorice. Set aside.

For the atomised fruits

Place the ingredients in the liquid nitrogen. Once they are hardened, beat them with care so that they break in small particles ('atoms'). Store in the freezer until used.

Pour a tablespoon of filling onto each apple slice. Sprinkle a pinch of sugar over them and caramelise slightly using a torch. Spread the atomized fruits, chopped chives and olive oil around them.

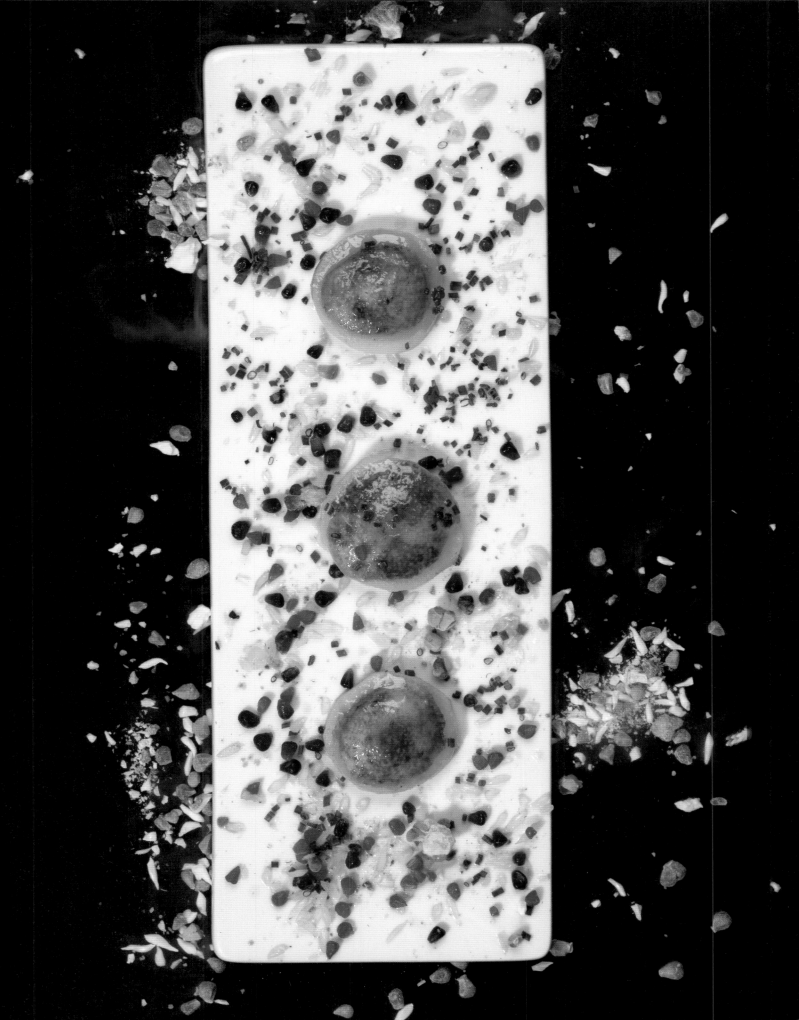

Foie with beer secrets

ingredients

4 people

For the foie gras

600 g foie gras
salt
black pepper

For the beer caramel

2 tablespoons water
40 g sugar
165 g beer
20 g yoghurt cream
40 g kefir

For the quince soup

250 g quince
500 g water
15 g tapioca
2 g sherry vinegar
salt

For the fresh almonds

30 g peeled fresh almonds
1 coffee teaspoon minced garlic
1 coffee teaspoon chopped parsley
salt

In addition

chives
malt powder
fried green pepper sticks

method

For the foie gras

Cut the foie in chunks of 50 g. Cook a la plancha very quickly just to form a nice crust. Then finish cooking in the oven. Season and set aside.

For the beer caramel

Slowly reduce the water, sugar and beer in a saucepan.
Once reduced and cold, mix with the yogurt cream and kefir.

For the quince soup

Blend the quince with the water for 5 minutes in a Thermomix and leave to stand in the chamber for 24 hours.
Strain the soup through a sieve, bring to the boil and add the tapioca, vinegar and salt.

For the fresh almonds

Sauté fresh almonds with garlic and parsley until slightly browned. Season.

Place the foie gras on a plate and draw a thick stripe of beer caramel on the right side of the plate.
Arrange 2 chives on the left.
Place the quince soup at the bottom.
Above and to the sides of the foie gras, place the almonds, green pepper, and remaining chives. Sprinkle the malt over the beer caramel stripe.

Cinderella with blue blood

Blue, violet, black Vitelotte or truffled potatoes, have very dark purple skins, but inside, when cut open, they are like water or grained wood with blueish streaks amid small, light and dark maroon ones, similar to cutting open a black truffle (hence one of their names). They are small, elongated potatoes. They are also known as Chinese truffles. The plant is very tall, the fruit is small and has beautiful white flowers with purple spots.

The genetic origin of this potato is unknown. It seems that, if anything, it is French, to be exact from the region of Brittany, and its culinary use is relatively recent, dating back just over 30 years. It is a variety of potato with more eyes, or buds, for reproduction. Its texture is very rugged and its flavour deep, like an old potato. It is rather starchy and somewhat sweet, more than the common potato (but not like sweet potatoes) and also with a slight nutty flavour. Its price is high due to low production. Like most varieties of potato, it is marketed throughout the year.

It is definitely a great idea to surprise people by using the blue potato instead of a usual potato. This potato is very versatile and a good garnish for any dish. It goes well with either red or white meats or fish. Almost everyone likes it and it can be prepared in many ways: boiled in water or steamed, fried, grilled...

Several haute cuisine restaurants use it as a garnish, mainly due to the spectacular colour it brings to the whole dish. As is the case, in puréed form, in the very modern version of ajoarriero in a glass at the thriving restaurant El Molino de Urdániz in Navarre.

Our recipe Blue Mallard Duck (a wild duck known by the same name) is accompanied by purée and sheets (or crystals) of this particular potato that goes beyond a pun. The truth is that this violet colour greatly embellishes the dish.

Blue mallard duck

ingredients

4 people

For the blue sauce

1 onion, gently sautéed
1 baked blue potato, without skin
2 slices fried bread
50 g fried almonds
25 g blue cheese
50 g vermouth
10 g virgin olive oil
salt
pepper

For the mallard duck

2 mallard ducks
salt
ginger
liquorice

For the sauce

2 duck carcases
3 medium onions
4 leeks
1 bouquet garni
200 ml olive oil
1 baked blue potato
chopped chives
oil from braising bones
salt
pepper
ground ginger

For the blue crystals

12 violet sweets

For the crisp blue potato sheets

4 blue potatoes
100 ml olive oil
salt
pepper
ground ginger

For the blue base

2 blue potatoes
50 ml olive oil
salt
pepper
ground ginger

In addition

borage flowers

method

For the blue sauce

Crush all the ingredients to form a thick paste.
Reserve.

For the mallard duck

Remove the duck breasts, season lightly and add a pinch of ginger and liquorice. Rub well with the sauce and cook a la plancha. Set aside. Use the rest of the duck to make the sauce.

For the sauce

Chop the carcases and brown in a pan with oil.
Separately, cut the vegetables and gently sauté in the rest of the olive oil until lightly browned. Drain well and add them to the carcases. Sauté well together and cover with water. Reduce, strain, season and add a pinch of ginger.
Separately, prepare a blue oil with the crushed potato and oil from the sautéed bones.
At the last minute, add a few drops of blue oil and chopped chives to the sauce.

For the blue crystals

Spread the sweets on a sheet of parchment paper, cover them with another and melt them in the oven. Stretch so that fine crystals are formed. Set aside.

For the crisp blue potato sheets

Cook the potatoes in the microwave wrapped in transparent paper. Peel and reduce them to a purée. Season and add a pinch of ginger.
Stretch this purée into very thin sheets, 8 x 8 cm, between two sheets of parchment paper. Dry at 60°C. Then carefully remove the paper and fry in oil at 115°C, without allowing them to colour.

For the blue base

Cook the potatoes in the microwave wrapped in transparent paper. Peel and reduce to a purée, to which add the olive oil. Season and add a pinch of ginger.

On one side of the plate, arrange the blue base, forming three little mounds. On each place a crisp sheet. Next to them the duck breast, lightly seasoned. In the central part, place violet crystals accompanied by some borage flowers.

Sublimation of flavours

Freeze-drying has been correctly defined 'as a process in which food, once frozen, is introduced into a vacuum chamber that separates the water by sublimation. Through different cycles of freezing-evaporating, it manages to eliminate virtually all the free water contained in the original product.'

The process of freeze-drying products – mainly in the food industry – begins once the raw material is harvested, prepared and immediately frozen, then passed into the freeze-drying process in a vacuum chamber. During this process, and under the influence of a slight warming, the water contained in the product in the form of ice is converted into steam and eliminated from the cells. The shape, colour, size, and consistency is preserved. The porous structure of the resulting cells in the final product allows for quick absorption of water when rehydrated.

The freeze-drying process retains the maximum flavour, vitamins, minerals, and aromas of the original product. Freeze-drying produces a completely natural product free from additives and preservatives.

An ancestral and, of course, very basic antecedent to freeze-drying arose out of necessity and a favorable environmental climate. For centuries it was used by the Incas and Vikings, who required high-calorie, lightweight food, that was easy to transport (low weight and volume) and did not rot, for their long journeys and military incursions.

The Incas took advantage of the high Andes with their icy nights and daytime sunlight to transform potatoes (papas) into chuño (made with potato starch) and llama meat into charqui (dried meat), carrying them in their backpacks – possibly the first products in history to be freeze-dried in a rustic and spontaneous way. The Vikings, with lower mountains and more oblique sunlight, freeze-dried herring with more imperfections.

Closer in time, researchers Bordas and d'Arsonval – in 1906 in France – and American Shackell in 1909, discovered the basic principle of sublimation, using elementary laboratory freeze-drying equipment.

Years later, industrial application began at the Pennsylvania School of Medicine in the works of E.W. Flosdorf and S. Mudd, who freeze-dried the first products for large-scale clinical use, mostly serum and plasma for the army.

Since then, the evolution of this technique has been spectacular, firstly for its almost exclusive pharmaceutical use and then, increasingly, in the food industry, where coffee and other soluble nutrients are at the forefront of freeze-drying.

And so we arrive at creative and modern cuisine, where the factor of conservation is less prized than that of taste. And a freeze-dried product not only maintains its properties intact but also strengthens and multiplies the factor of taste.

beans with chocolate and red tea

ingredients

4 people

For the bean truffle

70 g cooked white beans, well drained
10 g liquid cream
100 g white chocolate
8 g cocoa butter, melted

In addition

Freeze-dried red tea

method

For the bean truffle

Mash the beans into an extremely
homogeneous purée.
Melt the white chocolate and add the
ready melted cocoa butter.
Mix all ingredients and leave to stand
for three hours in the fridge.

Make balls with the mass of truffle
beans. At the last moment, cover
them in the red tea. Present the
truffles at room temperature.

mushroom snack

ingredients

4 people

For the mushroom broth

1 onion
1 garlic clove
½ leek
30 g olive oil
200 g mushrooms
50 g white wine
1 litre water
0.4 g xanthan gum
500 ml vegetable stock
25 g vegetable gelling agent
salt
pepper

In addition

20 g popcorn powder
30 g toasted ground almonds
2 g massala powder
2 g chopped chives
2 g chopped parsley
10 g freeze-dried mushroom

method

For the mushroom broth

Gently sauté the chopped vegetables in oil. When well browned, add the sliced mushrooms and wine. Leave to reduce and add the water. Simmer 45 minutes over low heat. Add the xanthan gum and crush together. Strain and add salt and pepper. Freeze in semi-spherical flexipan moulds. Set aside.

Separately, mix the vegetable stock with the gelling agent in a saucepan and boil for half a minute. When the temperature drops below 60°C, using a needle, dip the frozen half-spheres until they form an outer layer. Keep them cold (7°C) for a couple of hours, until the inside is thawed. Set aside.

Place the semi-spherical mushroom broth on a spoon and spread over it a mixture of prepared powders. Serve at room temperature.

an american, adopted son

When I first went to Mexico and discovered all types of different-coloured corn on the cob in the wonderful markets, I couldn't believe they were all edible, and thought the most striking were only used for decoration. The one I liked best, right from the beginning, was blue corn, one of the hundreds of varieties (red, black, white, even multicolour), which provides even more nutrition than yellow corn. This corn was traditionally used by the Hopi Indians, an Amerindian people who now live on the reserve of the Navajo people in Arizona. They used it to prepare for long trips or demanding work. In Mexico, they use blue corn in a dessert called Plato's Sweet, producing a sad, dull colour, and for this reason, this sweet is prepared exclusively for All Saints Day (Day of the Dead in Mexico). On less funereal dates, they make it with white maize. In Mexico, they also prepare a drink: mole poblano 'punch' made with blue corn and milk.

Corn is certainly not a very common ingredient in our European cookery, although today it is beginning to be a more familiar ingredient, especially in salads. But it still has a long way to go.

On the other hand, it's first worth noting that sweetcorn is the cob of certain varieties of maize, eaten as a vegetable. These varieties differ from fodder by their early maturation, smaller ears and higher sugar content, which provide the sweet taste, hence the adjective.

Unlike the fodder maize plant, which has been known for centuries, sweetcorn originated as a vegetable in the 19th century. It arrived in Europe after the Second World War. Today, it is increasingly popular and enjoyed.

We have spent many years in the kitchen and have returned many times to the subject of corn, which we have used in our restaurant in sauces, biscuits, tarts, aromatic oils, breadcrumbs, crispy coatings and veils, among other applications.

Thus, in a dish that we call 'Foie Gras Curd with Mango and Crispy Corn' (or quicos) corn is used as a garnish to decorate the dish at the last minute.

It is also very common in desserts. I remember a 'Terrine of Papaya and Tea with Sweetcorn Sauce', or a snack of 'Lightly-Seasoned Grey Mullet with a sheet of Fruit Compote and Tamarind Sauce', which had, as a base, some corn tortillas baked and then cut into rectangles.

And one of our best liked dishes that contained it – discreetly, but effectively – was the 'Parcel of Crayfish and Rice Noodles with Foie Gras Mayonnaise': at the bottom of the dish, embedded with the unique mayonnaise, we placed a prepared cake of mushrooms and cooked sweetcorn. Or in the striking 'Sheets of Begi Haundi in the Wind', the squid was coated in a mixture of powdered macadamia nuts and pulverized popcorn. Or in the expressively entitled, 'Corn Paving with Salmon'; as well as another very tasty snack 'Smoked Country House Chicken with Plum and Blue Corn' (dry and powdered as a coating for the chicken). Corn is already, without doubt, an adopted son of our cooking.

Foie gras with tejate

ingredients

4 people

For the duck foie gras

600 g duck foie gras
salt
black pepper

For the corn broth

300 g boiled sweetcorn
100 g vegetable stock
100 g truffle vinaigrette (1 litre peanut oil,
   150 g sherry vinegar, 260 g truffle juice)
22 g salt
¼ vanilla pod
25 g white chocolate
40 g organic corn oil
pinch of chopped oregano
salt
pepper

For the red fruit and spice coins

250 g water
5 g red fruit tea
1 g safflower
25 g vegetable gelatine
sugar
salt
black and white sesame seeds
safflower threads

For the cola sauce

200 g coca-cola
50 g crunchy corn
1 spring onion, cooked a la plancha
30 g olive oil
20 g fried bread
salt
ginger

For the chocolate corn

150 g dark chocolate covering
25 g crunchy corn

In addition

popcorn powder
celery sprouts

method

For the duck foie gras

Season the foie gras with salt and black pepper. Brown it in a pan and finish it with a salamander.

For the corn broth

Boil all ingredients. Remove the seeds from the vanilla and add them to the broth, removing the pod.
Purée and strain. Add the oil and oregano. Add salt and pepper.

For the red fruit and spice coins

Boil the water and infuse the tea and safflower. Add the gelatine and bring to the boil to set. Season and add a pinch of sugar. Place small spoonfuls of the preparation into a flexipan with coin-shaped moulds; decorate with a pinch of black and white sesame seeds, as well as a few strands of safflower. When cool, remove from the moulds and set aside.

For the cola sauce

Crush all the ingredients to a fine purée. Add salt and ginger.

For the chocolate corn

Melt the chocolate and coat the crunchy corn with it.

Arrange the foie gras escallops standing upright accompanied by the red fruit coins, the cola sauce and popcorn powder. Over this, sprinkle the chocolate corn and celery sprouts. Season separately.

Powder –

We have a product that's increasingly in vogue, very strange and innovative: maltodextrin.

Maltodextrin is a completely natural product. Specifically, a sweet carbohydrate obtained from cornstarch (also from wheat or barley) and usually found in the form of a creamy white powder.

It is digested more slowly than glucose and is therefore used as a sports supplement to attain more power when performing extended exercises. Many foods for children contain maltodextrin.

It has one small drawback that should always be made clear. Despite its low sweetening power, it is not suitable for diabetics or people intolerant of malt, nor for people with coeliac disease, as maltodextrin derived from wheat or barley may contain traces of gluten.

It is used as a bulking agent (increasing volume), but can also absorb oil. In the food industry it is used in the preparation of beverages, dairy products, soups, candies...

We began to use it in a culinary way to make a kind of white powder flavoured with oil. We mixed maltodextrin with virgin olive oil at room temperature to make a preparation that serves as the bed to a lobster. Visually it is very pretty and it is completely edible, of course, and tastes very good because, like pasta or rice, it has a great ability to absorb everything it touches.

The dish is brought to the table as a white blanket beneath the lobster and, when placed before the diner, an aromatic broth is poured over the white background, making a pleasant sauce. The white powder goes transparent and instantly becomes a delicate sauce.

As I say, it is very beautiful and rich. This is the first recipe that we created using maltodextrin as an ingredient, but we continued researching to find other formulas that worked with it, such as the texture of the crab puffs or some figures in the form of dolmens that accompany a bird as glorious as the turtle-dove.

white, pure and innovative

Lobster with extra-white olive oil

ingredients

For the lobster

12 lobster claws
salt
ginger
liquorice powder

For the lobster sauce

1 ripe tomato
1 tablespoon oil
flesh of 3 red peppers
50 g fried almonds
30 g bread, soaked in milk
3 tablespoons sherry vinegar
salt
ground ginger

For the extra white olive oil

50 g starch (extracted from tapioca)
30 g virgin olive oil

For the red safflower sauce

2 onions
4 tablespoons olive oil
100 ml red vermouth
2 litres chicken stock
1 g xanthan gum
safflower strands
salt
sugar
ground ginger

In addition

green of spring onions cut into thin rings
safflower strands
sunflower sprouts
red cabbage sprouts
a hint of lime

method

For the lobster

Lightly blanch the claws in boiling water, quickly cooling them in iced water. Carefully take away the shells and remove the meat intact.
Season it and sprinkle with liquorice and ginger. Reserve.

For the lobster sauce

Lightly blanch and peel the tomato. Cut into slices and pass them over a hot skillet with a tablespoon of oil to remove the touch of rawness.
Mix all the ingredients and crush finely. Season and add a pinch of ginger.

For the extra white olive oil

Mix the two ingredients at room temperature and set aside.

For the red safflower sauce

Clean the onions and cut into thin julienne and sauté in the oil. Once they are slightly caramelised, cover with the vermouth. Leave to reduce and add the chicken stock. Cook together over low heat for 30 minutes. Strain and add texture with xanthan. Add safflower and bring to the boil. Season and add a pinch of ginger, and sugar, if necessary. Set aside.

Coat the claws in the sauce and pass over the pan, back and forth, with a drop of oil. Season the claws with the red sauce and finish cooking on the salamander.
Spread the white olive oil on a plate to form a perfect square. Place the lightly seasoned lobster claws on it. Beside them, the cabbage and sunflower sprouts, safflower and spring onion rings. Grate a hint of lime on the surface.

Crab puffs

ingredients

4 people

For the puffs

400 g milk
4 g xanthan gum
30 g maltodextrine

For the anise and verbena preparation

100 g olive oil
30 g rice vinegar
3 g anise
3 g lemon verbena, finely chopped
a pinch of ginger
salt

In addition

100 g prepared classic San Sebastian-style
    crab

method

For the puffs

Emulsify all the ingredients in the Thermomix. Insert the preparation into a piping bag and make small mounds on a plate covered with a silpat.

Heat the oven to 190°C and put the plate in the oven. After 8 minutes, lower the temperature to 130°C and cook for 8 minutes. Cool and store in a dry place.

For the anise and verbena preparation

Mix all the ingredients and season.

Heat the crab. Make a small cut in the puffs and fill them with crab. Accompany with the anise and verbena preparation.

Turtle doves with dolmens

ingredients

4 people

For the doves

4 turtle doves
salt
ginger
liquorice

For the dove sauce

20 g whisky
35 g toasted pine nuts
2 g fresh basil leaves
3 g poppy seeds
100 g olive oil 0.4°
lemon juice
salt
pepper
powdered ginger
sugar

For the dolmens

100 g ground toasted almonds
60 g olive oil 0.4°
20 g ground poppy seeds
50 g maltodextrine
salt
pepper

For the sauce

4 dove carcases
½ garlic head, chopped
200 ml oil
1 aromatic bouquet
3 medium onions
4 leeks
salt

In addition

pea shoots

method

For the doves

Separate the breasts and legs from the doves, reserving the legs as a garnish. Season the breasts.

For the dove sauce

Blend all the ingredients together. Season. Rub the breasts and legs with the preparation and cook them a la plancha.

For the dolmens

Mix all of the ingredients to a firm mass that holds its shape. Make elongated figures (as shown in the picture).

For the sauce

Chop the dove carcase and brown in the pan with oil and garlic. Save a little of this oil to add to the sauce at the end. Separately, cut the vegetables and sauté in the remaining oil until slightly browned. Drain well and add them to the carcases. Sauté well, cover with water and reduce. Strain and season. At the last moment, add a few drops of the reserved oil.

Arrange the dove breasts upright with dolmens between them. Lightly sauce the breasts. Accompany with a few pea shoots and the fried legs.

it's gold, silver or bronze... that glitters

I love to surprise people, and the topic of gold, silver and other metals in cookery is certainly exciting. It is a great curiosity and important to know that metals can be edible and used in recipes, above all with great visual impact. To us this may seem new but they have been used in the cookery of half the world since time immemorial.

In ancient Egypt they added gold dust to conical breads that were closely associated with religious beliefs. Some images have been preserved in paintings, in which this sacred gold leaf is offered to the gods.

In China, the oldest documented references go back as far as 2500 B.C. Gold was used for medicinal purposes, as an elixir to prolong life. These superstitions still exist today in some small Chinese rural villages, where it seems they bake rice with a gold coin.

And in India, for example, where it is still popular today, gold and silver leaves, known as *varak* or *vark*, have been used for centuries to decorate desserts for celebrations, such as weddings or parties. Gold dust, known as *bhasma*, was used for numerous medicinal preparations and tonics to improve physical strength and memory.

In a festive ritual to celebrate the New Year, the Japanese mix sake and gold for good luck and prosperity (as we use grapes and the Italians, lentils). On the other hand, we have gold sushi or silver sushi with the makis rolled in gold or silver bread.

With regard to Europe in the Middle Ages, at the feasts of the nobility it was usual to serve large roasts covered with gold leaf. Gold was also widely used in cookery during the Italian Renaissance. For example, in 1386, Galeazzo Visconti, first Duke of Milan, apparently served a whole roasted calf wrapped in gold at the wedding of his daughter Violante.

Much more recently, the famous Italian chef Gualtiero Marchesi, mid-1970s cookery reformer in that country, had a dish that can almost be called historic: his risotto (already golden with saffron) was made even more magnificent with an excellent edible gold sheet that covered part of the dish.

Eating gold is not only for kings and I believe that, gradually, more and more products with gold will appear on the market. I know there are some chocolates and drinks (liqueurs and champagnes) in the marketplace containing gold. Neither gold nor silver adds flavour to a dish and are used mainly to embellish and, in some cases, to make one dish or another shine or sparkle.

As for bronze, it seems to be the third element . . . third in the scale of medals for prizes, but it has a colour and shine that I find appropriate to decorate and to bronze – not in the sun – but in some of our dishes.

Chocolate with emeralds and minerals

ingredients

4 people

For the chocolate coins

50 g milk
¼ vanilla pod
100 g dark chocolate
100 g half-whipped cream

For the emeralds

500 g water
60 g spinach
25 g parsley
salt
vegetable gelatine (per 250 g spinach
   broth, 12 g vegetable gelatine)

For the strata

2 egg whites
100 g sugar
25 g water
50 g crushed Marie biscuits
2 g star anise powder

For the vinaigrette

100 g green olive oil
1 tablespoon honey
3 g chopped parsley
few drops of sherry vinegar

In addition

edible gold dust

method

For the chocolate coins

Boil the milk with the vanilla and pour over the chocolate. Melt and leave to stand until it is cool enough to add the cream. Beat together, making sure that the mousse does not fall apart.
Pour the contents into a flexipan with coin-shaped moulds. Place in the freezer until needed.

For the emeralds

Boil the ingredients for 2 minutes and crush them finely. Drain and add the gelling agent in the appropriate proportion.
Using a hypodermic needle, dip the frozen coins to form a green film on the surface. Leave to stand.

For the strata

Beat the egg whites in a mixer until fluffy and add, little by little in the form of a thread, the syrup that was made with water and sugar to 116°C.
Beat until well risen and finally incorporate the biscuits and anise.
Mix carefully. Spread on a sheet of parchment paper and cover with another. Bake for one hour at 135°C. Break into pieces for serving.

For the vinaigrette

Mix all of the ingredients.

Place three chocolate emeralds on a flat plate. Arrange the strata beside them, making them higher than the rest. Add the vinaigrette and sprinkle with edible gold.

monkfish with bronzed onion

ingredients

4 people

For the monkfish sauce

100 g poached onion
45 g monkfish liver
50 g toasted pine nuts
25 g olive oil 0.4 °
25 g passion fruit juice
pinch of sugar
salt
pepper
ginger

For the monkfish

1 kg monkfish
salt

For the bronze oil

0.2 g edible bronze powder
100 ml olive oil

For the green chives

35 g fresh chives
80 g olive oil
salt

For the bronzed onion

500 ml water
1 onion
15 g sugar
0.3 g edible bronze powder
salt

For the sesame seed broth

500 ml chicken stock
8 g toasted sesame seeds
salt
pepper
powdered ginger

In addition

puffed quinoa

method

For the monkfish sauce

Crush all the ingredients to form a thick paste. Season with salt and pepper and add sugar and ginger to taste.

For the monkfish

Clean the monkfish, extract the loins, cut into portions, season and coat with the sauce.
Cook a la plancha, without giving too much colour.

For the bronze oil

Mix both ingredients.

For the green chives

Crush the ingredients to a green liquid. Season.

For the bronzed onion

Clean the onion and chop it. Cook in water with a pinch of salt.
Once cooked, blend with 100 g of cooking water, the sugar and the powdered bronze. Roll out into a thin layer on a silpat and allow to dry. Once dry, cut into irregular shapes, having heated it in the oven at 170°C until it is malleable.

For the sesame seed broth

Leave the seeds to infuse in the stock for 5 minutes. Strain. Season with salt and pepper and sprinkle a pinch of ginger.

Paint the monkfish with the bronze oil. When well coloured, arrange on a plate. Place beside it, the green chives and the broth. At the last moment, serve the bronzed onion and sprinkle on the puffed quinoa.

metal soup

ingredients

4 people

400 g milk
75 g cream
130 g sugar
1 vanilla pod
2 g silver powder
110 g kirsch

method

Boil the milk with the cream, sugar and vanilla in a saucepan for 2 minutes. Open the vanilla in half, remove the seeds and add them to the milk. Leave to cool. Once cool, add the silver powder and kirsch. Mix well in the mixer.

Present in crystal glasses, mixing before serving.

Duck with shot

For the duck paste

½ onion, gently sautéed
100 g coca-cola
1 garlic clove, fried
3 g dill
3 lettuce leaves (blanched in water)
50 g roasted nuts
50 sunflower kernals
juice of half a lemon
50 g virgin olive oil
salt
pepper
ground ginger

For the mallard duck

2 ducks (half bird per serving)
salt
ginger
liquorice

For the sauce

2 duck carcases
3 medium onions
4 leeks
1 bouquet garni
200 ml olive oil 0.4 °
chopped chives
oil from the braised bones
salt
pepper
sansho

For the shot

½ g silver powder
1 g eggplant ash
0.8 g xanthan gum
7.5 g gluco
225 g syrup (1 litre water and 225 g sugar)
50 g rice vinegar
25 g sherry vinegar

For dipping the shot

1.5 litres water
7.5 g alginate
200 g water
50 g sugar
25 g sherry vinegar

For the plant shot

100 g blue potato
100 g pumpkin
1 tablespoon olive oil
salt
pepper

For the wine salt

500 g sea salt
500 g red wine

For the dried fruit sand

40 g toasted Brazil nuts
25 g toasted macadamia nuts

In addition

small mint leaves
juniper berries

For the duck paste

Crush all the ingredients to form a thick paste. Add salt, pepper and a pinch of ginger. Set aside.

For the mallard duck

Remove the duck breasts and legs and lightly season with salt, ginger and liquorice. Spread with the duck paste and cook a la plancha. Set aside.
Use the carcases to make the sauce.

For the sauce

Chop the carcases and brown them in a pan with a little oil.
Chop the vegetables and sauté in the remaining oil until lightly browned. Drain away the oil and add them to the carcases. Sauté everything, cover with water and reduce. Strain and add a pinch of salt and pepper. At the last minute add a few drops of oil, chopped chives and a touch of sansho.

For the shot

Crush all the ingredients and leave to stand.

For dipping the shot

Completely dissolve the alginate in water (1.5 litres). Grind both ingredients and store in the refrigerator for 12 hours to remove excess air.
Add a 10 ml spoonful of the pellet preparation to the alginate and water solution. It is very important that the pellets do not touch each other, as they would stick together. Leave them in the solution for 3 minutes. Drain with a slotted spoon, taking care not to break them, and clean them in cold water. Drain again with the slotted spoon and reserve in the mixture of water, sugar and vinegar, until used.

For the plant shot

Remove small balls of potato and pumpkin with a Parisian spoon. Boil in salted water. Once cooked, sauté lightly in oil. Season.

For the wine salt

Mix both ingredients and spread them on a plate. Leave to dehydrate in a dry place.

For the dried fruit sand

Reduce both ingredients to powder, being careful not to grind them to a paste.

Sprinkle the dried fruit sand and wine salt in the middle of a plate. Place the duck breast on it, lightly sauced. Arrange the pellets, mint leaves and some juniper berries around this.

There exists a subtle difference between marinades and their first cousins mojos, mainly but not only, in the Canaries. Marinades were born as a medium for food storage, when there were no refrigerators, in the same way as Hispanic escabeche, salting, drying in the sun and air, or smoking. By contrast, mojos have always been less practical and more enjoyable.

As expressed in Canarian folklore: 'To sing well, you must eat grouper and roasted maize meal and scald your kisses with pepper mojo.' The various mojos, with their powerful base of garlic, paprika, cumin, coriander and chillies, green pepper and a long etcetera of accompaniments to fish and meat, although similar in composition and forcefulness to many marinades, tend to reveal the culinary habits of a people rather than the work of an effective preservative.

With technical advances, necessity becomes pleasure, and we no longer need to consider the conservative effectiveness of our marinades alone but to value above all the taste they contribute. Thus, as examples, we have the aroma of cumin, so Moorish, in Cadiz Bienmesabe or in marinated mackerel and, of course, the carnival 'pickled pork' or Embarrado from Extremadura.

Scalded kisses

Something else, definitely different but with a certain kinship to the mojo, is the Mexican mole. The history of the mole dates back to pre-Columbian times. The word itself, mole, *mulli* comes from Nahuatl, meaning 'sauce' (Nahuatl is a very ancient dialect in Mexico), meaning porridge or mix for the great lords.

However, (perhaps the most famous) mole poblano, which in its original recipe used about one hundred ingredients, was created for a feast in Puebla de los Angeles in the 17th century by mother Andrea of the Assumption, a Dominican nun at the convent Santa Rosa.

To be properly called mole, the dish must have at least fifteen ingredients, including chillies, of course. In Mexico there are a great variety of them, about fifty types. Each state has its own mole and the state of Oaxaca is known as the 'state of the seven moles'.

It is always best to prepare the mole the day before, and then add the turkey because it tastes better reheated. The reason is that the preparation is long and laborious, and the flavour is much improved when the different ingredients have time to integrate well. To make the mole paste, a metate should be used, a flat, heavy stone of volcanic origin, which used to be present in all Mexican kitchens, but is now unfortunately almost a museum piece. A modern robot or manual mill can be used.

ingredients

4 people

1 litre milk
250 g sugar
1 vanilla pod
8 egg yolks
75 g black mole

method

Boil the milk with the sugar and vanilla for
1 minute.
Off the heat, add the egg yolks to the milk,
and beat as if making crème anglaise. Heat
up to 70°C. Open the vanilla, remove the
seeds and add them to the cream.
Mix the mole with the previous preparation
and blend well.

Pass through an ice-cream batch
freezing machine and serve in a few
containers at a suitable temperature
(from -3 to -5 ° C).

black mole ice cream

bonito in a bonfire of scales and onions

ingredients

4 people

For the sauce of skins and scales

1 tomato
60 g bonito skin with scales (black)
30 g bread
2 spring onions, sautéed
200 g olive oil 0.4 °
70 g fried almonds
20 g balsamic vinegar
salt
sugar

For the bonito fillets

600 g bonito (150 g per serving)
salt
ginger

For the melon onions

2 medium spring onions
100 g melon
2 tablespoons olive oil 0.4 °
salt

For the gherkin broth

10 g parsley
70 g pickled gherkins, drained
500 ml water
60 g olive oil 0.4 °
15 g bread
salt

For the red pepper oil

10 g red peppercorns
60 g olive oil 0.4 °

method

For the sauce of skins and scales

Cut the tomato and quickly cook it a la plancha with a little oil. Separately, fry the bonito skins in half the oil until crisp. Drain well.
Mix all the ingredients. Crush and strain. Season and add a pinch of sugar.

For the bonito fillets

Cut the bonito fillets in rectangles. Of the 2 pieces per serving, one must be a little longer than the other. Smoke them lightly for 4 minutes in the smoker box. When the process is complete, season them, coat them with the sauce and cook a la plancha, keeping them juicy.

For the melon onions

Peel and halve the spring onions. Remove the interior part of the onion leaving only the outer layer.
Using a scoop, extract four melon balls and place one in each spring onion. Pass this over the oiled griddle plate so that it is well caramelised. Season.

For the gherkin broth

Crush everything. Strain and season.

For the red pepper oil

Vigorously rub the peppercorns together. Retrieve only the skins and mix with the oil. Set aside.

Place the bonito fillets upright in the centre of the plate. At their side, using a tube, draw some circles with the skin sauce. Arrange the spring onion on them (or off them, as in the picture). Lightly season the bonito fillets with pepper oil. Serve the hot broth in a separate container to accompany the dish.

Carabineros with a touch of morcilla

ingredients

4 people

For the dried morcilla wafers

two morcillas (500 g in total)
salt

For the morcilla sauce

50 g mashed roasted morcilla
  (prepared as in method)
dried tomato powder
star anise powder
salt

For the carabineros tails

12 carabineros tails
salt
black pepper
ground ginger
3 tablespoons olive oil

For the leek tears

50 g julienne strips of green leek
100 g leek broth (infuse with 1 g mace)
6 g vegetable gelatine
100 g virgin olive oil
15 g rice vinegar
salt
pepper

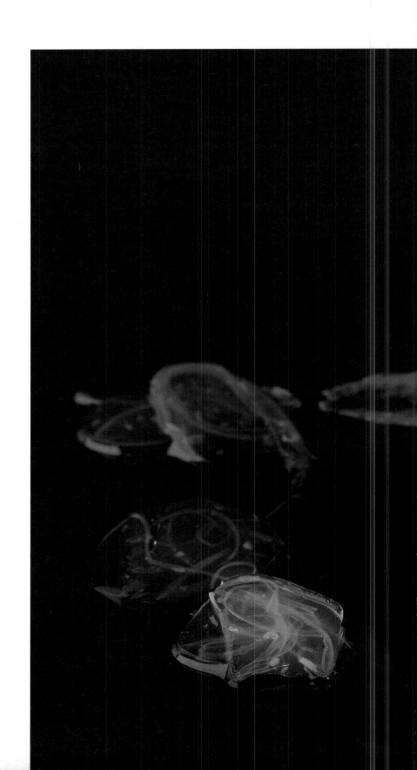

method

For the dried morcilla wafers

Bake the morcilla for 25 minutes at 190°C. Remove the skin and adjust the salt. Mash to form a purée. Keep back 50 g for the sauce.
Spread very thinly on a sheet of baking paper and cover with another.
Leave to dry at 60°C.
Once dry, cut into small wafers using a round cutter.
Reserve and keep dry.

For the morcilla sauce

Mix the 50 g of the morcilla purée, a pinch of tomato and the anise. Check the salt.

For the carabineros tails

Lightly season the tails and add a pinch of ginger. Rub them with the morcilla sauce and sauté in the oil. Set aside.

For the leek tears

Boil the broth, leeks and gelatine together. Season.
On a plate covered with a transparent paper, deposit a few teaspoons of the liquid, which, on cooling, will coagulate. Remove the leek tears from the paper and place them in the mix of oil and vinegar. Season.

Smear some morcilla sauce on the base of a shallow dish and stand the prawns on the sauce. Lean a wafer against each and drizzle with the leek vinaigrette tears.

Sea bass with beans

ingredients

4 people

For the sea bass sauce

50 g cooked white bean purée
20 g miso
5 g guindillas in vinegar
1 g angelica
10 g rice vinegar
salt
ginger

For the sea bass

4 sea bass fillets (125 g per serving)

For the red beans

180 g piquillo peppers
½ clove garlic, chopped
2 tablespoons olive oil 0.4 °
120 g water
1 g angelica
5 g gelatine
salt
sugar

For the green beans

250 g zucchini (courgette)
25 g spinach leaves
1 g zahareña (*sideritis angustifolia*)
5 g gelatine
salt

For the white beans

140 g cauliflower
120 g milk
100 g cream
1 g cumin
5 g gelatine
salt
pepper

For the bean sauce

250 g white bean cooking broth
80 g white wine
25 g soy sauce
10 g maple syrup
1 g sage
salt
pepper

In addition

wild onion sprouts
sunflower seed sprouts
2 tablespoons parsley oil

method

For the sea bass sauce

Crush all the ingredients to form a thick paste. Season and add a pinch of ginger.

For the sea bass

Spread with the sauce and cook a la plancha. Set aside.

For the red beans

Sauté the garlic with oil in a saucepan. As soon as it begins to colour, add the piquillo peppers (without seeds) and sauté together. Pour in the water and add the angelica. Leave to cook for 5 minutes, crush and strain. Season and add a pinch of sugar. Using 5 g of gelatine per 100 g of prepared sauce, blend the piquillo pepper sauce with the gelatine and bring to a boil. Pour into bean-shaped moulds. Leave to cool.

For the green beans

Wash the zucchini and spinach. Chop the first and cook both ingredients in boiling water. Once cooked, drain the vegetables and reserve 250 g of the cooking water. Crush the water, zucchini, spinach and zahareña. Strain and season.
Per 100 g of the zucchini preparation, add 5 g of vegetable gelatine. Blend the zucchini preparation with the jelly and bring to a boil. Pour into bean-shaped moulds. Leave to cool.

For the white beans

Wash the cauliflower and chop it. Cook with milk, cream and cumin. Blend and strain it. Add salt and pepper. Per 100 g of cauliflower, add 5 g of vegetable gelatine. Blend the prepared cauliflower with the jelly and bring to a boil. Pour into bean-shaped moulds. Leave to cool.

For the bean sauce

In a saucepan, reduce by about 70% the mixture of wine, soy sauce, maple syrup and sage. Once reduced, add the bean broth. Cook for 5 minutes over low heat. Remove the sage and add salt and pepper.

Remove the coloured beans from the moulds and use three of each colour per plate. Mix with parsley oil until ready to use.
Spread a small spoonful of sauce in the centre of the plate and arrange the sea bass on it. Place beans, with the oil, around the fish. Intersperse between them the wild onion and sunflower sprouts. Accompany the dish with the remaining sauce.

Leaves
that do not fall

It cannot be said that the use of leaves in culinary tradition is strange. Of course, I mean leaves from all kinds of trees and shrubs, and not those from plants or green vegetables, which have been our daily bread for centuries.

It seems we are forced to do what the Greeks have been doing since time immemorial, which is to take advantage of vine leaves, creating an interesting mezze, known as Dolmadakia or Dolmades, essentially vine leaves stuffed with minced meat and rice.

Nearer to hand, in Murcia, there is a dessert typical of the area, Paparajote, a really genuine Murcia delicacy... lemon leaves coated with batter, basically made with flour and egg, fried and sprinkled with sugar.

With exactly the same lemon leaves, brought directly from the orchards of Murcia, we developed a dish of red mullet in our restaurant, using lemon leaves to flavour them. That was in the Seventies. As long as the dish stayed on the menu, these leaves were graciously sent to me by my dear friend Raimundo González, the major force behind the modern Murcia culinary scene and founder of the legendary El Rincon de Pepe.

Today in our new dishes, we use this type of leaf in a different way, infusing them to make a vinaigrette or sauce. At first, we did this with olive leaves. Everybody knows that the olive tree (*Olea europea*) is widely cultivated throughout the Mediterranean for the production of olives and our essential everyday olive oil. However, we noted that in the Middle East, it was used for centuries as a type of tea or an olive leaf infusion for the treatment of sore throats, coughs, fever and to improve health generally. Furthermore, it has a unique and pleasant taste. Finally, our steps led us to the leaves of another – so-called multipurpose – tree, the walnut, which produces fruits and nuts, which are highly appreciated in our area and, in particular, in my Basque country.

And, indeed, it occurred to us to deconstruct a typical cider dessert that we dared to call: 'Eggs (by the way, it is really a mixture of two cheeses, fresh and Idiazábal), Cider and Walnut Leaves (in infusion)', also with a detail of caramelised walnut fruits.

eggs with cider and walnut leaves

ingredients

4 people

For the eggs

500 g cream cheese (yogurt type)
100 g sugar
200 g mango flesh
25 g small cubes of smoked Idiazábal cheese

For the egg dip

1 litre water
5 g alginate (purified substance obtained from seaweed)

For the cider

250 g cider
50 g walnut leaf infusion
50 g sugar
3 g xanthan gum

For the caramelised walnuts

50 g walnuts
40 g sugar
1 tablespoon water

In addition

pansy petals cut into julienne strips
pinch of leek ash
pinch of freeze-dried orange peel powder

method

For the eggs

Firstly mix the sugar with the cream cheese to form an homogeneous mixture, and then separately mix the mango flesh and cheese cubes.

For the egg dip

Completely dissolve the alginate in water. Mix both ingredients and keep the product in the refrigerator for 12 hours to eliminate excess air.
Place in a 15 ml spoon, a spoonful of the cream cheese and, over it, the mixture of mango flesh and Idiazábal. Pour the contents of the spoon into the alginate and water solution. It is very important that the 'eggs' do not touch one another, as they will stick together. Leave in the solution for 3 minutes. Drain with a slotted spoon, without breaking them; clean in cold water. Set aside until used.

For the cider

Cold mix all the ingredients in a blender. Leave to stand for 5 hours in the refrigerator to eliminate excess air introduced in the blender.

For the caramelised walnuts

Mix the sugar with the water. Heat and let the sugar dissolve to make a syrup. Add the nuts and keep at a steady temperature.
Stir continuously with a wooden spoon so that the nuts are caramelised uniformly. Remove the nuts from the heat when all the liquid has evaporated. Leave to cool on parchment paper.

Drizzle the cider on the bottom of a dish. Arrange the eggs and nuts on it. Decorate with the ash, orange peel powder and the fine julienne of flowers.

a paper, without paper

It is quite probable that this statement is confusing: 'Fruit and vegetable paper'. However, linguistic license allows us to use it with some freedom, and not as a purely literal proposal.

The confusion refers to the fact that we think we can use paper to cook products. A great cooking technique from France: the papillote (from *papillon* or butterfly, by the way), basically consists of wrapping food in flame retardant paper or wattle (as in years gone by) or aluminum, and cooking it in the oven at a medium temperature.

Here we refer to something quite different. In some cases simulating the true skin, for example of a fish, with a few thin sheets that resemble paper, or, in another case, creating a visual illusion like festive confetti. But in both cases, the paper is actually made from fruits or vegetables.

A few years ago at the restaurant, we began to prepare a type of pimiento skin for some fish we serve as an appetizer.

At first this idea arose because we wanted to serve portions or strips of marinated 'erla'. But they lacked the skin that fish have and that we sometimes love to eat. We decided to make a really pretty, shiny red skin, like that of many rich fish, which, of course, would be succulent and with a flavour to accompany the fish.

We decided to make it like a new skin, with thin red slices of piquillo peppers. Really, there is no secret to this. It is very simple. I think it is one of those achievable preparations that can be made with ease in any home. We work with professional machines, but it can be done with the usual things in a normal kitchen.

First a few quality piquillos are chosen and crushed with a little salt and sugar to obtain a smooth, thin cream. This cream is spread between two sheets of baking paper and crushed until quite thin and then left to dry at 60°C. (We do this in a machine that we have for this purpose, but at home it can be dried in the oven.) Finally, we cut it to the size of the portions of fish.

Beauty and flavour. We work a lot with this theme of sheets and it allows us to play about, contributing to the surprise factor, always providing a lot of fun and breaking our predictable routine.

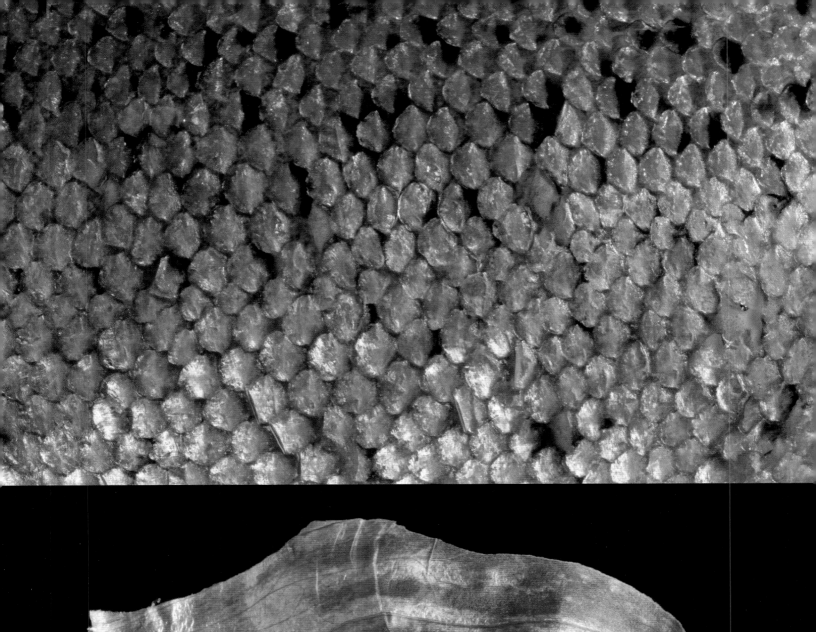

redcurrant paper

ingredients

For the redcurrant paper

300 g dried redcurrants
500 g water

For the sharon fruit

2 ripe sharon fruit
100 g red vermouth
30 g sugar

For the orange blossom water infusion

100 g water
10 g rose petals
10 g sugar
3 g orange blossom water

4 people

method

For the redcurrant paper

Boil both ingredients for 10 minutes over low heat. Crush together to a smooth paste. Spread between two sheets of parchment paper until very thin. Dry in the oven at 50°C for 12 hours. Peel away both papers and reserve.

For the sharon fruit

Peel the sharon and cut in four. Vacuum pack with the other ingredients. Cook at 65°C for one hour. Stop the cooking action with ice water and leave them in their individual bags. Set aside.

For the orange blossom water infusion

Boil the water with the sugar and infuse the rose petals. Leave for 5 minutes and filter. When cool, add the orange blossom water. Set aside.

Open the sharon fruit bags. Wrap the fruit chunks in the redcurrant paper. Moisten them with the orange blossom water infusion. Serve at room temperature, to eat in one or two bites as a pre-dessert.

Amber of anchovies

ingredients

4 people

For the red anchovy

1 tin piquillo peppers
salt
sugar

For the anchovies

12 anchovies
salt
olive oil

For the orange sauce

25 g olive oil
25 g orange, without membrane, finely
    chopped
2 g fried garlic, well chopped
5 g pickled gherkins, chopped
3 g rice vinegar
salt
sugar
powdered ginger

For the spiced cellulose

1 vanilla pod
2 g aniseed
fennel leaves
5 g starch
400 g water

For the fatty sauce

100 g tocino (pork fatback)
3 drops balsamic vinegar
chopped parsley
salt

method

For the red anchovy

Chop the peppers thoroughly. Season with salt and sugar. Spread the mixture between two sheets of paper and leave to dry at 60°C. Once dry, cut into slices the size of anchovy fillets.

For the anchovies

Clean the anchovies, leaving them in two fillets. Cover with salt for 30 minutes. Remove the salt and place them in olive oil.

For the orange sauce

Mix all the ingredients well and add salt. Reserve the mixture.

For the spiced cellulose

Open the vanilla pod in half and cook it in the water with the aniseed for 5 minutes. Blend with the starch and add fennel leaves. Leave to cook for a minute. Remove the vanilla pod and spread the mixture thinly between two sheets of paper. Leave to dry at 60°C. Set aside.

For the fatty sauce

Sauté the tocino and leave to cool. Chop with a knife to form a paste. Add the chopped parsley and vinegar. Season.

Cover the anchovies on the skin side with the dried pepper.
Put four coffee spoons of fatty sauce on the bottom of a shallow dish;
arrange three red anchovies on this and another wrapped in on itself in the
form of a package. Wrap the spiced cellulose over this last one. Drizzle the
dish with orange sauce.

ingredients

4 people

For the sea bass in schisandra brine

4 sea bass fillets (125 g per serving)
500 ml schisandra infusion (*Schisandra sinensis*)
30 g fine salt
olive oil

For the sea bass sauce

1 onion
1 leek
1 clove of garlic
15 g fried bread
10 schisandra berries
50 g olive oil
salt
pepper

For the red confetti

24 piquillo peppers in oil
salt
sugar

For the green confetti

180 g spinach leaves
salt

For the potato with red and green paper

100 g boiled potatoes
3 anchovies in olive oil (canned)
5 green Ibarra chillies
pinch of chopped parsley and sage
salt
pepper

For the schisandra broth

¼ chicken
100 g cooked meat
1 onion
1 bouquet garni (leek, parsley, thyme, carrot)
2 g schisandra
1 g salvia
salt
pepper

In addition

sage leaves
schisandra berries

Sea bass with vegetable confetti

method

For the sea bass in schisandra brine

To prepare the schisandra infusion (500 ml of water, 10 g schisandra flowers), boil the water and add the schisandra off the heat. Cover and leave to stand for 5 minutes. Strain.
When cold, thoroughly dilute the salt in the schisandra infusion. Add the sea bass fillets to the infusion and leave to sit for 25 minutes. After that time, lightly dry with kitchen paper and momentarily dip them in the sauce and cook them a la plancha with a drop of oil. To finish cooking, preserve them in olive oil. Set aside.

For the sea bass sauce

Sauté the vegetables with a dash of olive oil. Add the remaining ingredients. Crush and add salt and pepper.

For the red confetti

Grind the peppers to a homogeneous paste. Season with salt and sugar. Spread the mixture very thinly between two sheets of paper and leave to dry at 60°C. Once dry, cut with a stationery cutter for making confetti. Save the remaining red sheets.

For the green confetti

Cook the spinach leaves in salted boiling water. Drain well and mash thoroughly, checking the salt. Spread the mixture between two sheets of paper and leave to dry at 60°C. When it is dry, cut it with a stationery cutter for confetti. Save the remaining green sheets.

For the potato with red and green paper

Roughly chop the anchovies with the chillies. Stir in the cooked potato and crush with a fork, to make a purée. Add the sage and parsley and season the mash.
Wrap it in the leftover green spinach and red pepper sheets to form a few stuffed tubes.

For the schisandra broth

Loosely cover all the ingredients, except the anise, with water and cook for 3 hours over low heat. Skim as it begins to cook and whenever necessary. Strain.
Make an infusion with the schisandra and sage. Strain and add salt and pepper.

Place the sea bass in a soup dish, accompanied by the infused broth. Pour the confetti, schisandra berries and sage leaves over the sea bass. Place stuffed tubes alongside.

Don't even leave the leftovers!

It is very traditional to serve fish dishes as well as meat dishes with their spines and bones. There's nothing so delicious as sucking the crispy bones of a grilled turbot or the bone of a good chop. A fine Hispanic saying very expressively indicates how good a dish has been when: 'Sucked to the bones'.

Bones, especially when crisp, as with anchovies, fried or in garlic; the aforementioned turbot with cartilaginous parts, or sea bream (the prized gelatineous morsel is its eyes), or sucking the bones at the nape of hake and other fish. But eating the bones or the hard cartilaginous parts is more unusual, and is currently under research in our kitchen, where we have developed many ideas with regard to this.

For example, the feathers of crispy squid in a dish of squid, the backbone of a bonito from the north, minted and crunchy, or a very tasty snack, prepared with many technical skills on a base of grilled prawn heads.

My close associate Xabier Gutiérrez in his book *The Culinary Forest* says: 'We do not need to go to any other country to be told that the best part of a prawn is the head, which holds all the aromas, juices and essences of the animal. But it is true that they (referring to the East) taught us how to do something with the head of a prawn.'

As historical background to the theme of edible bones in Spanish cuisine, we remember scraps of fried anchovies: a small masterpiece of kitchen scraps, thanks to the departed Josep Mercader of Hotel Empordà in Figueres (Girona), who, many years ago, transformed leftovers into a small masterpiece in a very addictive appetizer, which has become famous throughout Catalonia and half the world.

As for the use of fish skin, this has been a recurring theme in cookery, particularly in roasts. The skins of bream, turbot, bass, sea bream etc, have been greatly valued, not only in the role of conserving meat and fish, but also for their characteristic taste, when smoked and grilled. Indeed, we could say that a majority of these fish, without their skins, lose many of their features. Not to mention mullet and hake itself, which, like it or not, keeps its skin in many recipes for this reason.

The crispy skin of many fish is very rich, and sometimes it is used to give colour to the dish. In some recipes, fish skin allows us to make important sauces like pil pil. This recipe would not be the same if we cooked the cod without its skin.

Balanced sole

ingredients

4 people

For the sole

2 sole, 400 g each
olive oil 0.4 °
salt
powdered ginger

For the sole skin

the skins of the sole
200 ml olive oil 0.4 °

For the sole paste

50 g hazelnut butter
30 g lettuce leaves, coloured on the griddle
  plate
10 g dry squid
15 g cooked white beans
1 tablespoon sherry vinegar
20 g meat stock
salt
pepper

For the sole sauce

500 g beef consommé
1 g lemon grass
1 onion, gently sautéed
2 g xanthan gum
salt
white pepper

In addition

shiso sprouts
cream of balsamic vinegar

For the sole

Clean the sole, reserving their skins.
Cut them in half, following along the backbone. Cut the halves to get four pieces. Season and add the ginger. Set aside.

For the sole skin

Stretch each skin fully on a sheet of parchment paper and cover with another. Cut into pieces 12 x 4 cm and fasten to both sides of a wave-shaped metal mesh. Fry them in oil. Remove the mesh and set aside.

For the sole paste

Blend all of the ingredients. Season with salt and pepper and reserve.

For the sole sauce

Fully dilute the gum in the consommé. Simmer all the ingredients over low heat for 5 minutes. Drain and season.

method

Rub the sole with the paste and fry in a frying pan with a little oil so that it colours on both sides and stays very juicy. Remove the spine and rub a pinch of paste in the middle of the fillets.
Place the sauce in the bottom of a shallow dish and, above it, the crispy skin standing upright. Place the sole over the latter. Garnish the dish with a few drops of balsamic vinegar and shiso.

monkfish with lead and bone

ingredients

4 people

For the monkfish paste

100 g onion, gently sautéed
45 g monkfish liver
50 g toasted pine nuts
25 g olive oil 0.4 °
25 g passion fruit juice
salt
pepper
sugar
ginger

For the monkfish

1 kg monkfish
olive oil
salt

For the monkfish marrow and spine

the main monkfish bone
olive oil

For the vegetable threads

the skin ½ aubergine (eggplant)
½ beetroot
4 tablespoons olive oil

For the sauce

2 onions
1 green pepper
500 ml water
25 g monkfish
15 g monkfish liver
2 tablespoons olive oil 0.4 °
salt
pepper
ginger

In addition

tomato powder

method

For the monkfish paste

Crush all the ingredients into a thick paste. Season and adjust with a pinch of sugar and ginger.

For the monkfish

Clean the monkfish and remove the fillets, reserving the backbone. Cut into portions. Season the monkfish and smear with the paste. Cook a la plancha with oil without allowing too much colour.

For the monkfish marrow and spine

Cut the monkfish backbone longitudinally in two halves with the help of a cutter. With a fine spoon extract the marrow found in the joints of the two half spines. Set aside. Meanwhile, cut the two half spines into thin slices and fry over low heat until crisp.

For the vegetable threads

Cut the vegetables into fine julienne all the same size and keep them in olive oil.

For the sauce

Clean the vegetables and cut into strips. Once gently sautéed, add the monkfish meat and sauté. Add the water and simmer for 20 minutes. Mash along with the liver, and strain. Boil the sauce and add a pinch of salt, pepper and ginger.

Arrange the monkfish leaning against the fried spine. Drop the drained vegetable threads around the monkfish and spread the sauce at the base. Place the marrow at the side of the monkfish. Sprinkle on the tomato powder.

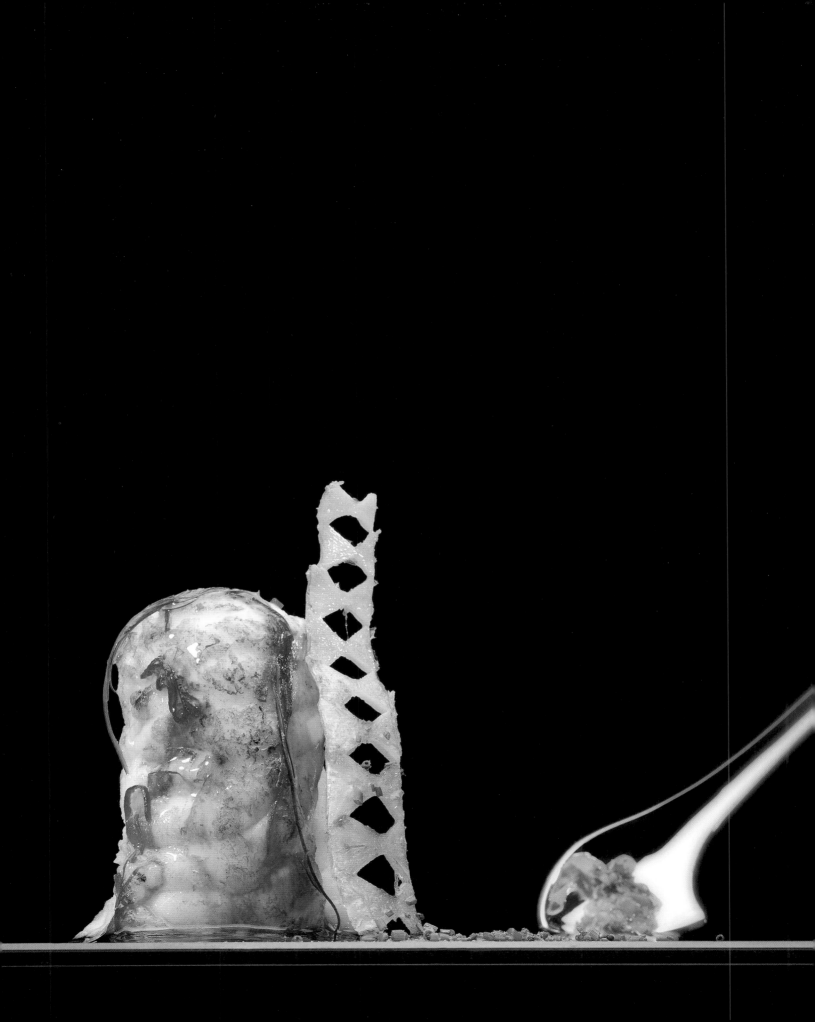

and to dust you shall return

We have repeated ad nauseam that drying was one of the first methods used for food conservation, taking advantage of periods of abundance to keep reserves for times of scarcity.

Various drying methods have been discussed elsewhere in this work, but I believe it is worth pausing over something we use extensively, no longer for food conservation, but to give taste and lift to a sauce or main dish.

It's traditional to use dried foods, crushed very finely to powder, especially spices.

Paprika is obtained by very finely crushing dried red peppers. To look at other cultures, far away but increasingly becoming near, wasabi is powder made from the dried root of Japanese horseradish, or garam masala, typical in India, is a powder made from crushing different spices. In these foods, crushed when dried, with the water removed, the flavour is greatly concentrated, as is the aroma when the powder is kept tightly closed in appropriate containers.

Years ago, the Navarre chef Jesús Sánchez, in his Cantabrian restaurant El Cenador de Amós, in a star dish that is still on the menu (Fillet of Cod Roasted with Mushroom Flour and a Light Beef Gravy) 'breaded' the spine of the fish with a powder, which is nothing but dried and powdered mushrooms.

In our establishment, both in our research and daily cooking, different powders are increasingly used to flavour vinaigrettes as wells as sauces, and also to sprinkle on top, providing colour, aroma and taste. Not only is this mere aesthetics, which of course it is, but it also affects the depth of taste. For example, one of our first dishes using a powdered product – a deconstruction of traditional Basque cuisine – was: 'Hake in Green Sauce and Vinaigrette of Clams Sautéed with Ham Powder'. An important flavourful contrast for so delicate a fish as hake. Not only with the marine elements (clam vinaigrette) but also with the powdered ham.

There are other powders: of vinegar, wine, black olives, tea, tomato, ginger, not to mention the classic cocoa or different spices and dried herbs.

Our menu also had a dish of oysters with powdered almonds. And a San Pedro or Muxu Martin fish, accompanied by an hibiscus sauce, garnished with a powder of cheese bark and ham with cinnamon.

The vinegar powder we used is the same as the one that is added to sushi (therefore, a Japanese product), sold ready-made in specialist shops (especially for oriental cookery) and its function is to fix the flavour, and we have enough evidence of this (some sweet meringues were made too sweet), while, unlike liquid vinegar, it does not easily curdle when in contact with cream, egg yolks, beaten egg whites or dairy. It can also acidify biscuits or reinforce acidity, as a contrast to fatty fish.

Rattles

ingredients

4 people

100 g macadamia nuts, chopped
20 g butter
10 g filo pastry
10 g tomato powder
10 g almond powder
2 litres olive oil
salt
pepper

method

Brown the chopped macadamia nuts in a
little butter. Set aside.
Place four nut pieces in square flexipan
moulds. Fill with olive oil and freeze for
one day.
Unmould and wrap the frozen tablet in a
sheet of filo pastry.
Fry in plenty of oil until golden.
Sprinkle with tomato powder, salt, pepper
and almond powder.

Given that the frozen oil will melt
during frying, the filo pastry will
be wrapped around a few pieces
of macadamia nuts, which upon
shaking, resemble a rattle. Serve
hot.

Mimetic sole

ingredients

4 people

For the sole

1 sole, 800 g
olive oil 0.4 °
salt
powdered ginger

For the sole side flaps

the sole side flaps
100 ml olive oil 0.4 °
salt

For the sole paste

100 g fried almonds
2 g aubergine ash
1 onion, gently sautéed
½ garlic clove, fried
20 g coconut
40 g lemon juice
150 g cava
salt
pepper
ginger

For the sole sauce

500 g chicken stock
1 g poppy seeds
1 onion, gently sautéed
2 g xanthan gum
salt
white pepper

For the mimetic powders

wild amaranth powder
pinch of of eggplant (aubergine) ash
freeze-dried tomato powder
powdered ginger
freeze-dried parsley powder
tandoori

method

For the sole

Clean the sole and fillet it, removing the four fillets. Reserve the outer sole fins and spines to be used as garnish.
Season and add the ginger. Set aside.

For the sole side flaps

Fry the side flaps in the oil. Completely drain away the oil and season.

For the sole paste

Blend all of the ingredients. Season with salt and pepper and reserve.

For the sole sauce

Dilute the xanthan gum well in the stock. Simmer all ingredients over low heat for 5 minutes. Strain and add salt and pepper.

For the mimetic powders

Keep them separate and in a dry place until the last moment.

Rub the sole with the paste and lightly fry in a pan with a little oil, lightly colouring both sides, keeping it juicy. Try to ensure the sole keeps its length and does not shrink.
Place the lightly seasoned sole fillet on a plate and sprinkle it with different powders, creating a mimetic scene that simulates the habitat of the sole in the sea. Accompany it with the sauce and the fried side flaps.

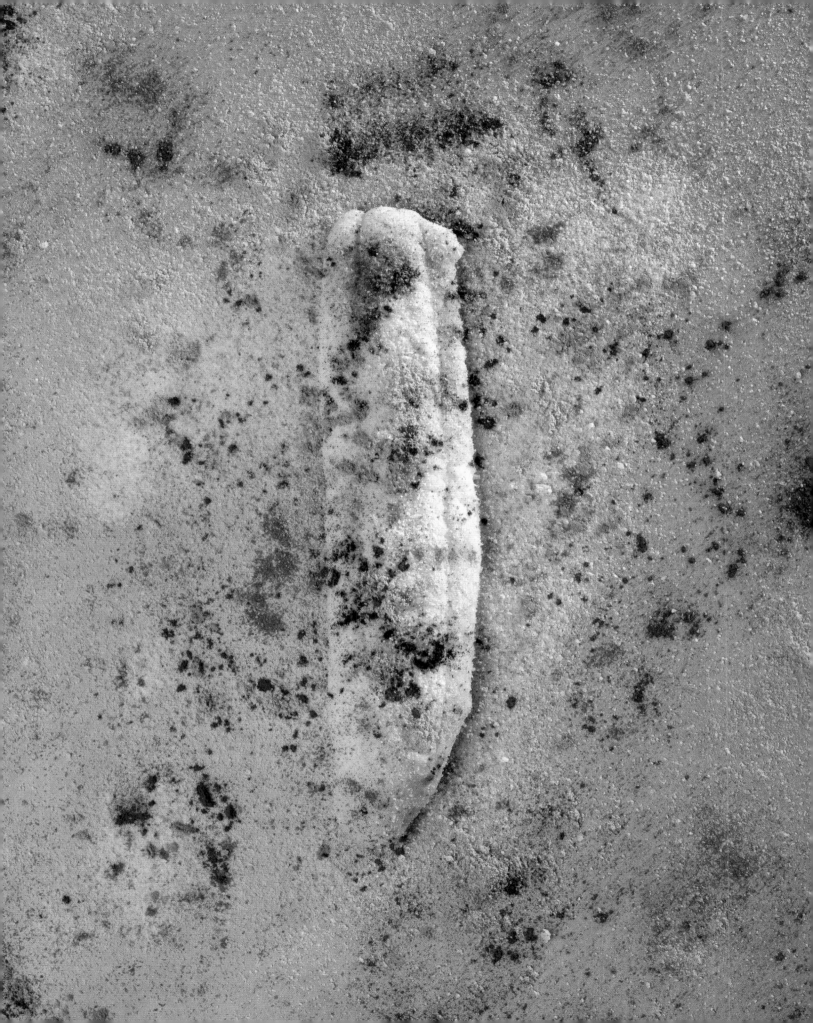

The subversion of colour

In a paper (at Madrid Fusion 2009) expressively entitled 'Colour is also a Flavour', presented by my daughter Elena and the research team with Xabi Gutiérrez and Igor Zalakaín, lies the key to the use (among other natural dyes) of red beetroot (whose vivid colour, thankfully, possesses the powerful pigment betacyanin) and, at the risk of being very synthetic, it can be summarised as follows.

We all know that the presentation of meals and their colour combinations, plated more and more artistically, play an essential role in the most up-to-date cookery, of course, always with the prerequisite of flavour. But precisely in this sense, we can venture much further, thanks to a psychological aspect, not at all secondary, that colour influences and even determines the sense of taste or flavour to an extent almost similar to the texture of food. This is because the sight of food (an essential part of which is its colour or combination of colours) stimulates the desire to consume, to the extent that we have come to create the apt phrase 'eat with your eyes'.

In addition, we usually instinctively associate each colour (along a secular process embedded in our cultural memory and collective personal taste) with a particular taste. Specifically, we Basques immediately associate black with squid in its own ink. Therefore, to present squid in red ink subverts the concept most deeply rooted in our cultural culinary heritage, although, basically, it does not vary much in flavour to squid prepared in their own ink.

Of the product used for this disruptive metamorphosis, red beetroot is a food that we cannot do without, and not just for its colour. It is highly valued in the modern culinary kitchen for two fundamental reasons: its sweet flavour in contrast to other salty, sour and bitter flavours in a dish and, of course, as a colour contrast. You need only see the beauty it brings to a dish. It can be shown together with the gold of oil, colouring a vinaigrette red. Or, in contrast to the green of spinach or parsley, and even dyeing scarlet a bird as wonderful as a bleeding dove or covering a chocolate and olive oil truffle in a purple veil. Colour is also flavour.

Scarlet dove

ingredients

4 people

For the dove preparation

4 doves
salt
pepper
powdered ginger

For the dove sauce

2 dove carcasses
3 medium onions
4 leeks
1 bouquet garni
200 ml olive oil
1.5 g powdered mace

For the dove paste

dove livers
dove hearts
50 g cooked beetroot
20 g almond paste
25 g red wine
10 g sugar
10 g balsamic vinegar
1 g mace
salt
pepper

For the 'scarlet' beet

500 g water
100 g beetroot
0.5 g mace
salt

In addition

sunflower shoots
garlic sprouts

method

For the dove preparation

Remove the bird breasts and season lightly.
Set aside the livers and hearts for making
the paste.
Use the carcasses and other cuts to prepare
the sauce.

For the dove sauce

Chop the carcasses and brown them in a
pan with a little oil. Once sautéed, reserve
some of the oil.
Separately, chop the vegetables and sauté
in the remaining oil until lightly browned.
Drain and add to the carcasses. Sauté well
together, cover with water and reduce.
Strain and season. At the last moment, add
a few drops of the reserved oil and the
mace.

For the dove paste

Crush the ingredients together to form a
thick paste. Add salt and pepper.

For the 'scarlet' beet

Peel and chop the beets. Cook them in the
water and mace for 20 minutes.
Crush both ingredients and lightly season.
Spread on a silpat and leave to dry. Once
dry, remove and chop irregularly. Set aside
(no need to store in a dry place).

Coat the breasts with the paste and
cook a la plancha, leaving them
very juicy.
Place the breasts on a plate and
make a cut at the base so they can
stand. Place a pile of dried beet in
front of them with the sprouts on
both sides. Drizzle over the sauce
in such a way that it catches the
beetroot and looks like red
blood from the doves.

Squid in red ink

ingredients

4 people

For the squid

12 small squid

For the squid in red ink dressing

2 g minced orange peel
2 g chopped lemon zest
100 g raw beet juice
25 g virgin olive oil
pinch of white sesame powder
chopped parsley
salt
ginger
sarsaparilla powder

For the squid filling

25 g fresh corn kernels
3 tablespoons olive oil
25 g diced papaya
1 onion, gently sautéed
salt
pepper

For the black sauce

100 g squid ink sauce (classic)
30 g raw beetroot juice

For the pickles and carambola broth

5 g parsley
1 carambola (star fruit)
15 g pickled gherkins, drained
250 ml water
30 g olive oil 0.4 °
8 g breadcrumbs
15 g fried almonds
salt
sugar

method

For the squid

Clean the squid and separate the bodies and tentacles. Save the ink for preparing the black sauce.
Open the bodies in half and make several cuts on the squid, but not through them.

For the squid in red ink dressing

Mix all the ingredients except the squid and tentacles.
Place the squid in this mixture for 10 minutes. Then place the tentacles in for 5 minutes.
Fry the squid in a hot pan with a dash of oil to brown them slightly.

For the squid filling

Grind the corn with the oil and strain.
Mix all the ingredients and season.

For the black sauce

Separately bring the two ingredients to the boil and mix them.

For the pickles and carambola broth

Crush well and strain the whole. Season and add a pinch of sugar. Heat before serving.

Arrange the squid bodies and tentacles on a plate wrapped round the filling.
Using a crumpled cloth, previously spread with the squid and beetroot sauce, trace irregular spots on the plate.
At the last minute drizzle on the gherkin and carombola broth.

beet with chocolate and olive oil

ingredients

4 people

For the beet veil

1 cooked beetroot
salt
sugar

For the olive oil truffle

225 g cream
50 g glucose
340 g dark chocolate
80 g virgin olive oil

In addition

1 tablespoon virgin olive oil

method

For the beet veil

Thoroughly mash the beet to a purée. Add a pinch of salt and sugar. Spread it in a circle between two sheets of paper, forming a thin layer, and leave to dry at 60°C. Once dried, remove the papers.

For the olive oil truffle

Chop the chocolate and slowly add it to the hot mixture of previously boiled cream and glucose, in order to absorb it. At the last moment, add the olive oil.

Rub the veils with olive oil to add brightness. Wrap half a tablespoon (soup spoon) of olive oil truffle in each veil.
Serve at room temperature.

Candles and a boot

A truly fascinating subject is the use of both wax and resin in the kitchen.

Wax is a fatty substance secreted from the glands of young worker bees. They use it to make honeycombs and to seal the cells when they are filled with honey.

The wax used here is that which walls up the cells, to be exact, the lids. When this wax is removed, it contains honey, pollen, propolis and some impurities (the remains and legs of bees). But everything contributes to the flavour of the wax. In fact, when you visit honeycombs, the beekeeper offers you a piece of honeycomb to chew, like chewing gum, until only the wax stays in your mouth, and you end up spitting it out. This is the honey and wax flavour that we wanted to achieve. We wanted to incorporate the pleasant aroma of the smell of natural wax candles in a dish. To most people this may seem a rare ingredient, but I can assure you this flavour is present in many sweets and candies. As to types of dish, wax is as often an ingredient in savoury as well as sweet dishes. We spent a long time developing a wax ice cream, where wax is involved in the preparation of the cream for the ice cream.

We also came up with a more complex dish that we initially called, 'Wild Duck (also made with pigeon outside the hunting season) with Lost Wax'. The poultry is prepared with sauces or salsas of honey and pollen, but a gel with oil and wax is separately prepared. When served, a piece of wax gel is placed on one side of the dish (previously cooled, so that it does not spread). This wax gel melts at the table, in front of the customer, with the help of a small torch. The olfactory sensation caused by the smell of melting wax is very pleasant. This melted wax mixes with the juices and the sauce accompanying the bird.

On the other hand, historically, resin is perhaps more related to gastronomy, and more specifically to the world of wine. Firstly, there is the very traditional taste associated with artisan 'boots' or skins that, for centuries, have been used for wine conservation, incorporating resin, a substance extracted from pine forests, which is treated to remove its flavour, and then placed on the skin or 'boot'. On the other hand, the taste of resin is not only for conservation, as is typified in some wines from Greece, for example, Retsina, which is a white wine that must contain at least 85% of the native variety Salvatiano, to which pine resin is added. Adding substances to wine, including resin, dates from ancient times, and the taste for it has remained on Greek palates to the present day.

Pigeon with beehive wax

ingredients

4 people

For the paste

100 g apple purée
1 fried garlic clove
25 g fried bread
50 g fried almonds
5 g honey
15 g Dijon mustard
60 g olive oil

For the pigeon

two pigeons (525 g per serving)
salt
ginger
liquorice

For the sauce

2 pigeon carcasses
3 medium onions
4 leeks
1 bouquet garni
200 ml oil
2 tablespoons acacia honey
salt

For the freeze-dried wax

200 g milk
50 g cream
50 g beeswax
15 g honey
2 g pollen

For the gel wax

125 g sunflower oil
20 g wax
1 g salt

method

For the paste

Blend the ingredients together to form a thick paste.

For the pigeon

Remove the pigeon breasts and season lightly with salt, ginger and liquorice. Rub well with the paste and cook a la plancha. Set aside. Reserve the carcasses for making the sauce.

For the sauce

Chop the carcasses and brown them in a pan with a little oil.
Separately, chop the vegetables and sauté in the remaining oil until lightly browned. Drain well and add to the carcasses. Sauté together, cover with water and reduce. Strain and season. Add a few drops of oil at the last minute.

For the freeze-dried wax

Boil all the ingredients in a saucepan. Once boiled, leave to cool. The wax will form a layer on the surface of the container. Strain the whole. Freeze the mixture and insert in the freeze-drier. Leave to freeze-dry.

For the gel wax

Heat all the ingredients to 69°C. Set aside in the fridge.

Place some sauce and the breast on a plate, accompanied by the freeze-dried wax without touching the sauce. To one side place some gel wax, on an area of the plate which will have previously been cooled. In front of the diners, and using a culinary torch, proceed to melt the gel wax. When it melts, it will release its aromas and join with the body of the sauce.

tacos with aged beef and 'boot' wine

ingredients

4 people

For the aged beef

360 g loin of aged beef (4 servings of 90 g)
salt
black pepper

For the veal sweetbreads

1 veal sweetbread
½ leek
½ carrot
few drops of vinegar
salt

For the propolis paste

40 g toasted bread
1 g propolis
30 g olive oil
30 g chicken broth
salt
pepper
powdered ginger

For the 'boot' wine sauce

150 g wine marinated for 72 hours in a
   wine 'boot'
20 g sugar
0.5 g xanthan gum

For 'boot' wine air

200 g wine marinated for 72 hours in a
   wine 'boot'
10 g sugar
4 g soy lecithin

For the potato with propolis

1 potato
200 ml olive oil
pinch of propolis powder
salt
pepper

In addition

propolis powder

method

For the aged beef

Season and set aside.

For the veal sweetbreads

Clean the sweetbreads and scald with a few
drops of vinegar.
Cook together with the vegetables and a
pinch of salt for 6 minutes.
Then remove and leave to cool, out of the
cooking juices.
Cut the sweetbreads into rectangles.

For the propolis paste

Crush all the ingredients together and
season.

For the 'boot' wine sauce

Mix everything in a blender. Leave to rest to
recover the colour.

For the the 'boot' wine air

Beat everything together with a small whisk
until bubbles appear on the surface.

For the potato with propolis

Cut the potato into rectangles
approximately 1.5 cm thick. Make some
holes on the surface to fill with the 'boot'
wine.
Season the potato and sprinkle lightly with
propolis powder.
Preserve in oil.

Rub the tenderloin and
sweetbreads with the paste and
roast on a charcoal grill.
Arrange the meat and
sweetbread with the potato
alongside. Spread a little wine
sauce and wine air. Sprinkle
with propolis.

milk puff pastry with wax

ingredients

4 people

For the milk puff pastry

500 ml milk
pinch of icing sugar and powdered yoghurt

For the white custard

500 ml milk
100 g sugar
1 vanilla pod
4 g kuzu

For the wax ice cream

1 litre milk
100 g cream
200 g beeswax, finely chopped
6 egg yolks
300 g sugar

method

For the milk puff pastry

Cover the surface of a non-stick pan with the milk and reduce until practically burning. Using a spatula, collect the adhering milk and sprinkle with the yogurt and icing sugar mixture.

For the white custard

Dilute the kuzu in the milk and boil with the sugar and vanilla. Halve the vanilla, remove the seeds and add them to the milk.

For the wax ice cream

Boil the milk with the cream and the finely-chopped wax. When it boils (without moving, in order not to dirty the sides of the saucepan), allow it to cool to 40°C. The wax will have solidified and can be filtered. Add the egg yolks, beaten with the sugar. Heat to 82°C, stirring constantly. Transfer to the ice-cream machine.

Present the ice cream in a dish, covering the surrounding area with the milk puff pastry. Drizzle with custard.

the
poetry
of food

It is well known that food flavouring is a discovery that dates as far back as the Neolithic era. Salt was initially used by chance but, when it was first deliberately added to food, it caused the second culinary revolution. The first was the cooking of food.

There are many stories about the importance of salt in the past that sometimes go unnoticed but that endorse the significance of this ancient condiment. In classical Greece, Homer mentions it as something divine, and tells us that the Trojan heroes always ate meat seasoned only with salt.

Salt was a symbol of hospitality in Rome. Jesus said to the Apostles: you are the salt of the Earth. The Church has used salt in baptism as a symbol of incorruptibility. The word salary comes from the Latin, because Roman troops were given part of their pay in salt. And the Phoenicians in Spain taught much about salt, especially as an element of conservation, mainly for salting fish.

Such was the importance of salt that it was subjected to taxes, controlled by the most powerful in the land, was the cause of wars and stimulated extensive trade.

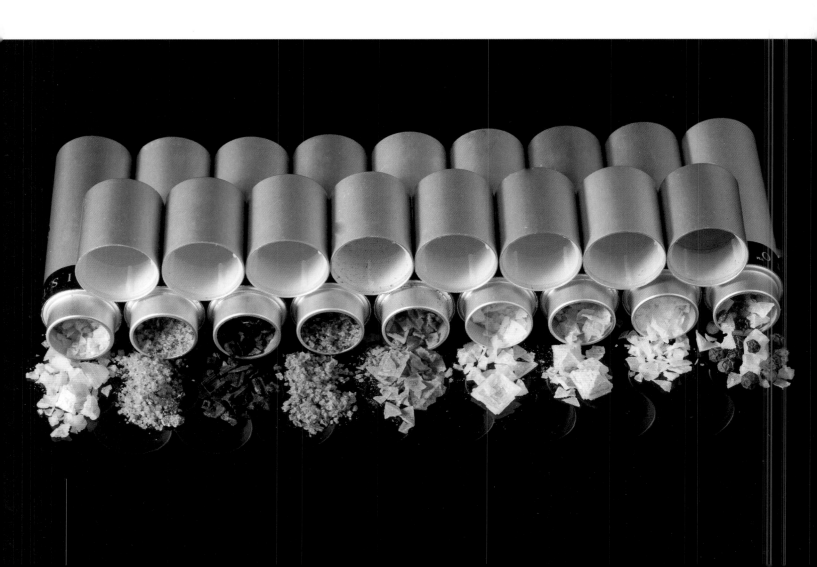

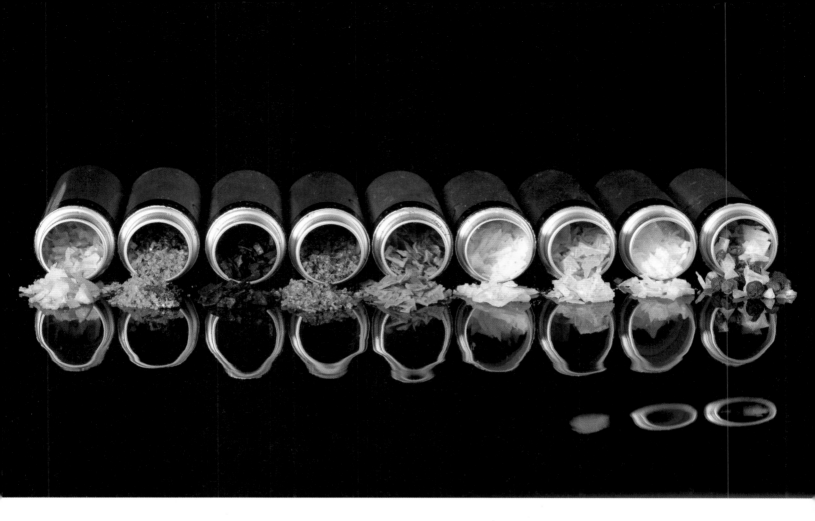

Moreover, the word sauce or salsa, which defines a more or less liquid dressing, either hot or cold, accompanying a dish or used to cook it, comes from the Latin: *salat*. That is, it tells us that salt is the basic ingredient of all sauces. A very beautiful saying goes: if meat, fish or rice and other foods are the prose element of meals, spices and condiments are their poetry.

But to understand the history of salt, we must remember that besides preserving food out of necessity, salt is, above all, a food flavouring, which adds strength to the taste of the food it seasons and also provides the body with sodium and chlorine, helping to maintain the balance of body fluids.

As San Isidoro de Sevilla said: 'There is nothing more necessary than salt and sun.' Today, in the marketplace there are a countless number of salts: sea or land (from salt works or mines), coarse and fine, rocky, or as delicate as flowers, white or grey, natural or mixed with other aromatic elements, flavoured, delicate or powerful, and more or less rich in nutrients.

Without doubt, the most outstanding are: English Maldon sea salt, coarse Baleine sea salt from the French Camargue (highly fluoridated and iodized), and salt from Guérande. Of the latter, located in Brittany, there are two types: the grey, medium grains rich in magnesium, and fleur de sel, which is white and harvested by hand.

As for English Maldon sea salt (from Essex), it is the flower of exquisite salts, which like great harvests, doesn't occur every year, since it needs special weather conditions favouring the deposit of a thin layer of flat crystals on saline waters, that visually remind us of frozen flakes.

But there are other curious salts: smoked, which gives the quirky touch of smoke without the hassle of the usual process. There is also a curious salt, sold as samphire, off the French Opal coast, which is nothing but twigs of the most evocative sea vegetable, salicornia. In the same vein, we have very fashionable gomasio, a mixture of salt with dried seaweed. And, of course, an almost endless range of salts with flavours and aromas, ranging from orange, dried tomato, truffle, vanilla or green tea, and even more curious wine, olives, squid or ham.

Today more than ever, salt undoubtedly adds poetry to meals, even the most prosaic.

tough
lifeboats

Harold McGee, a scholar of world recognition, a genius especially on food chemistry and cooking, in his monumental encyclopedia *On Food and Cooking* (with a prologue to the Spanish edition by the biochemist Unai Ugalde and my young and admired colleague Mr Andoni Luis Adúriz) quite rightly tells us: 'seeds are our most durable and concentrated food. They are tough lifeboats designed to carry the descendants of a plant to the port of a distant future.' It is undoubtedly a synthesized

But many other seeds adorn and enhance a lot of our recipes. Most of these seeds come from far away. Thus, mustard seeds have been found in prehistoric caves both in Europe and in China, and have been cultivated for two thousand years. It is logical that they are cited both in the Bible and in Greek and Roman literature. The Greeks held them in such high esteem they believed that Asclepius (God of Medicine) had discovered them, and a paste made from mustard seeds is mentioned by Pythagoras (about 530 BC).

But there are others that we must not forget, such as coriander seeds, cumin, millet and sorghum, anise, juniper, or the sweet and almond-shaped poppy seeds.

explanation, filled with poetry but at the same time rigorously scientific. Later, in a clairvoyant way, the author demonstrates the nutritional and culinary value of the same, noting that: 'as ingredients, seeds have much in common with milk and eggs. All are composed of basic nutrients created to nurture the next generation of living beings; all are relatively simple and of little taste by themselves, but they have inspired cooks to transform them into some of the most complex and delicious foods we have.'

From purely culinary experience, we can confirm that all of this is very true and that seeds are part of many of our dishes, not so much for their nutritional value but for that very unique touch they provide, however small and simple they may seem. The magic of a bread with sesame seeds undoubtedly makes it outstanding, complex... different.

We can find sesame or sesame seeds (small oilseeds) untoasted, toasted, ground with salt, called gomasio, in the paste called tahini, in oil, mixed with aromatic herbs etc. Starting with our local seeds, whether white, gold or black, their most common use is to complement or enhance a dish or contribute a grainy and crunchy texture.

The near and the far

This headline undoubtedly fits splendidly when we talk about a product like soy sauce which, beginning as a rather exotic and distant stranger among us, has become, along with other products initially exogenous to our cuisine, a truly adoptive child.

The soya bean fashion was introduced more than three decades ago by the French reform movement, in particular by one of its then young and rebellious chefs, the most 'Asian' of all, Louis Outhier, then chef at L'Oasis restaurant at La Napoule in the heart of the French Riviera.

But salted and fermented soya beans are among the oldest Chinese flavourings. A liquid called *jiang* – antecedent to this sauce – was used more than 2,500 years ago. The current sauce started to be used widely in the 6th century.

Essential in Chinese and other Asian cookery, this dark sauce is made by fermenting soya beans with flour and water. This then goes through a process of distillation and aging. The sauce combines roasted soya beans with ground grain, usually wheat, with a special mould of yeast and brine, causing the development of lactic acid bacteria similar to yogurt. The resultant mixture, called moromi, is left to age for some time. This reddish brown semi-liquid mass can be left up to two years (it is said for two summers) continuing the process of fermentation, during which it acquires its oiliness, aroma and characteristic flavour. After this, the solids are separated from the liquids by a process of pressure, strained through different cloths, and the pasteurised liquid is packaged in small bottles, that look like perfume. There are essentially two types (although in Japan there are up to six varieties): one, with increased aging, more intense colour and stronger, sweeter flavour, called 'superior soy sauce', is used to accompany dishes. The other, lighter, softer and more savoury in taste, is more often used for cooking.

It is curious that soy sauce, which was born as a food preservative, has in the end become a real pleasure. However, as with other foods, its original use had a lot to do with religion. And in particular with the spread of Buddhism in China and Japan, since many of its followers became vegetarian, creating the need for a seasoning without a meat base, so they experimented with this paste made from cereals and fermented soya beans.

marinated meat

ingredients

4 people

For the tenderloin

500 g tenderloin
kombu
ground pepper

For marinating the tenderloin

1 litre soy sauce
300 g sake
20 g sugar
30 g rice vinegar
3 g powdered yuzu

In addition

onion shoots
2 hot peppers in vinegar, chopped
2 pickled gherkins, chopped
virgin olive oil
ice flakes

method

For the tenderloin

Clean the meat of fat and sinews. Add
ground pepper and wrap in the kombu.

For marinating the tenderloin

Mix all the ingredients and cover the loin
with them. Leave to marinate for 72 hours.

Remove the meat from the liquid and pat
dry with a cloth. Then cut the tenderloin
into 1cm thick fillets and lightly fry
them, on one side only, in a very hot
pan. Arrange the fillets on the ice flakes,
placing them on the side that was fried
in the pan. Arrange the shoots, peppers,
gherkins and a trickle of olive oil on a
dish and, finally, the meat.

ingredients

4 people

For the chicken

1 chicken breast

For the chicken marinade

200 g soy sauce
2 garlic cloves, crushed
10 g sweet paprika
50 g brandy
pinch of oregano

For the pear cubes

1 pear
1 soup spoon olive oil
pinch of powdered ginger

In addition

2 soup spoons olive oil

Chicken pear

method

For the chicken

Cut the chicken breast into bite-size pieces.

For the chicken marinade

Mix all of the ingredients. Marinate the chopped chicken breast in the mixture for 12 hours.

For the pear cubes

Peel and core the pear. Cut into cubes and sauté in the oil. Sprinkle with ginger.

Brown the chicken pieces on both sides in a hot pan with oil. Pierce the diced pear and chicken with a fork and present them standing as shown in the photo.

the forest
on a plate

I believe the use of soil in some of our dishes has created quite a stir, as expected. And it is because it is amusing, shocking, and even, why not say it, rather daring. But ultimately, it is essentially talking about and dealing with the odours and aromas of the forest, especially in autumn . . . for some time now we have been working with soil, with compost. We came up with a very interesting recipe a few summers ago, and presented a dish called 'composted squid'. Our research began when we opened up a laboratory. We started working with 'earth' and thinking about tastes and aromas.

For example: Mushrooms? What do they taste of? What do they smell of? Truffles? What is their essential taste? And what is the olfactory memory of their wonderful and intoxicating aroma? Abstracting ourselves from the products, closing our eyes, the effluvia in all that we tested brought forth a similar response: the smell, above all, of earth, compost, and, of course, something inherent in forests, especially in autumn: leaf litter (we use the word *orbela*, which means litter in Basque).

The answers to these elementary questions were interesting to study. But we all also wondered: What can we do with this?

We decided to make a very unique fumé – then use it to soak a bed of vegetables, which we used almost like a broth.

In the first place, a good selection of raw material was needed (of course, soil of the forest, without pollution or waste). It was infused in boiling water and treated as if it were any other aromatic herb. Then it was strained (passed through a fine sieve) to obtain a brownish broth, brimming with the deep aroma of the forest.

We first used it in the above-mentioned 'composted squid', and the truth is that, after initial misgivings, a lot of people liked it. The name surprised them but the flavours were familiar. It is highly reminiscent of earthy fungi, mushrooms, truffles etc. It is as if we have taken a piece of nature and served it up on a plate. In this case, rather than being in 'sea and mountain', or 'surf and turf', the squid in the abstract is in sea and forest.

begi haundi squid in the abstract

method

For the squid a la plancha

Clean the squid and separate, to one side, the wings and tentacles and, to the other, the bodies.

Open the bodies in half and cut into 6 cm squares and make several cuts on the squid without cutting right through. Marinate them for 12 hours in the garlic oil, salt, orange, ginger, a pinch of chopped parsley and sarsaparillo powder.

Cook the squid fillets a la plancha until they take on a pretty golden colour.

To make mushroom powder, cut a few mushrooms into thin slices and dry them in the oven or any other ventilated source at 60-65°C. Once dry, reduce them to dust with a crusher.

Sprinkle with the dried mushrooms, chopped parsley and a few strands of safflower.

For the earth sauce

Bring the composted earth up to the boil in the water. Remove from the heat and leave to infuse for 5 minutes. Strain through cheesecloth.

Clean the vegetables and cut into julienne strips. Sauté gently in the olive oil. Once well-sautéed, add the mushrooms and chopped squid meat. Sauté well and then incorporate the well filtered infusion of earth and water.

Cook for 15 minutes. Crush and strain. Season with salt and pepper, and add a pinch of mushroom powder.

For the oiled parsley and earth sauce

Lightly mix all ingredients and add the olive oil at the last minute. Keep the sauce well-oiled. Add salt and pepper.

ingredients

4 people

For the squid a la plancha

1 large squid (*begi haundi*), 700 g
25 ml garlic oil
8 g orange peel, dried and chopped
ginger
sarsaparilla powder
5 g mushroom powder
pinch of chopped parsley
safflower threads
salt

For the earth sauce

60 g composted earth
1.5 kg water
3 onions
1 leek
100 g squid meat (fins, legs, etc.)
50 g mushrooms, cleaned
pinch of mushroom powder
olive oil
salt
pepper

For the oiled parsley and earth sauce

10 g earth sauce
500 ml olive oil 0.4 °
4 g orange peel, chopped
pinch of mushroom powder
chopped parsley
salt
pepper

In addition

sage flowers

Arrange the squid fillets, standing in the centre of the plate, leaning against each other. To their side, dot the oiled parsley and earth sauce. Draw a line of earth sauce with a small roller (used for painting). Garnish with sage flowers.

bacon without sorrow

Among many exotic, strange and amazing products, we can also speak about ancestral foods that avant-garde cookery does not depreciate, but rather improves by applying innovative techniques, adapting them to today's tastes with imagination and sensitivity.

Bacon is one such, and it is at its very best when this fatty meat comes from Iberian pigs.

On the other hand, like many other food terms, the word bacon comes from the Old French word *bakko*, ham, which came to denote a piece of salt pork or the whole hog. In fact, in ancient times, a state banquet, serving only pork was dubbed a 'bacónica meal'. What happened is that the English soon took ownership of the word and now, when speaking of bacon, we immediately think of Anglo-Saxons. However, the passion for bacon and *torreznos*, which are fried and crispy pieces of bacon, has a long tradition in Spain from centuries ago.

There are even beautiful literary references, specifically from Cervantes, who includes in the regular diet of a genial gentleman, the poetic 'sorrow and damage'. Apparently this dish, which was made with corned beef, bacon, sausage and eggs, could only be eaten on Saturdays because according to an old Castille custom (which ended up being abolished by Pope Benedict XIV in 1742), no fresh meat or suet could be eaten on Saturdays, so they took the opportunity to consume corned beef, prepared with cattle that had either died or been killed while migrating or in pens. Apparently, the odd phrase 'sorrow and damage' refers to the pain this caused the owners of the herds, who lost their animals, and the fact they used to break the bones to take advantage of the marrow in soups and stews, hence the 'damage'. Furthermore, cured meat or smoked pork was used by old Christians to distinguish the Jews, who on Saturdays ate *adafina*, composed only of lamb or beef, and for whom pork was a forbidden and sinful animal, as it was for the Moors, as well. That is why, as the saying goes, 'Bacon has many enemies from the Moors to fine people'. Speaking of sayings, one that is indeed very macho in this respects, is: 'Bacon makes the pot, man the marketplace and woman the house'.

Tocino crystal with hake cheeks and strawberries

ingredients

4 people

For the hake cheeks

8 hake cheeks
salt

For the leek, strawberry and pepper mixture

2 leeks
6 strawberries
6 green chillies in vinegar
2 tablespoons olive oil
salt
pepper

For the tocino slices

500 g tocino (pork fatback)

For the ham stock

600 g serrano ham, in pieces
500 g water
3 g agar agar

For the tomato seed vinaigrette

seeds of two ripe tomatoes
10 g truffle juice
10 g sherry vinegar
40 g olive oil 0.4 °
zest of half an orange
salt
powdered ginger

For the strawberry air

strawberries
salt
pepper

In addition

flower petals and buds

method

For the hake cheeks

Season the hake cheeks and at the last moment before plating, cook lightly a la plancha.

For the leek, strawberry and pepper mixture

Clean and finely chop all the ingredients. Sauté the leek in oil, without letting it brown. Once soft, add the rest of the ingredients and lightly stir-fry over high heat. Add salt and pepper.

For the tocino slices

Machine slice several rectangular tocino slices the size of the hake cheeks.

For the ham stock

Lightly fry the ham pieces in a pan and pour in the water. Leave to simmer until reduced to 300 g of broth. Dilute the agar agar in the broth. Add a pinch of salt and spread out on a flat plate. Cut the gelatinized broth in thin rectangles.

For the tomato seed vinaigrette

Mix all the ingredients well. Season and add a pinch of ginger.

For the strawberry air

Liquidize the strawberries and lightly season with salt and pepper.
If the liquid is too thick, add a little water. Beat the liquid with a small whisk until foam forms on the surface.

First, arrange the leek mixture as a base for the hake cheeks. Spread the tocino slices over the hake cheeks, covering them. Place the thin ham broth gelatine on the tocino slices. Heat the dish in the salamander to warm the gelatine. Drizzle with tomato seed vinaigrette and top with strawberry air.

Magical spheres

Xanthan gum (or simply xanthan) is a relatively recent product, used since 1969. It was developed in the United States as part of a programme to find new applications for maize, as it is produced by fermentation of the sugar, which can be obtained previously starting from cornstarch, by the bacterium *Xanthomonas campestris*. Xanthan gum is simply a gelling agent, i.e. a natural product that allows us to modify the original texture of a liquid to achieve a greater density. It comes in a powder and its dosage depends on the density of the original liquid and the texture we want to obtain.

Its easy dissolution, stability at almost any temperature, and the fact it does not confer flavour but gives a pleasant or, at least, neutral taste sensation, means that it is used to increase viscosity in countless sauces and commercial products.

In cookery, xanthan gum has very interesting applications. On the one hand, it can be used as a thickener to thicken sauces in a simple way, without the flavour sometimes added by other traditional thickeners (flour, tapioca, potato...), which tend to be much heavier. In addition, very colourful effects can be achieved with it. In transparent or translucent liquids, it can be used to keep small pieces of solids in suspension, while not producing any colour: for example: with a fruit salad in a glass of fruit juice, small pieces of fruit can be distributed throughout the volume of the glass, as the density of the liquid prevents the pieces from rising to the surface. In fact, this effect was used commercially in drinks before renowned chefs began to use it. What is amusing is to introduce coloured liquid droplets into transparent or translucent liquid. The different densities do not mix (or take a long time to do so) and the density of the xanthan gum prevents the droplets from rising, so they stay suspended inside the liquid.

My friends Ferrán Adrià and his brother Albert are the chefs who have researched and written most about this gelling agent, one of the products we can now begin to use in a spherical way. Stepping further into the world of contemporary cuisine, they have even marketed a Spherification MiniKit (with alginate, gluco, xanthan gum, agar and Lecite, a soy lecithin-based emulsifier), with which you can experience – even at home – all those textures offered by the more daring chefs. These starter kits for molecular home cooking can create a wide range of dishes with great diversity of flavour and texture, based on the spherification technique.

Sugared bread and champagne

ingredients

4 people

For the champagne bread

100 g dry bread, cut into small squares
300 g milk
190 g lemon jam
100 g water
60 g sugar
60 g champagne

For the champagne veil

200 g champagne
30 g sugar
3 g kappa

For the sugar crust

375 g sugar
25 g egg whites
spice powder of different colours (paprika,
  parsley, curry, dried raspberries etc.)

For the champagne

200 g champagne
30 g sugar
3 g xanthan gum

In addition

orange zest
orange skins
courgette, in small cubes
campanula (flower)
begonia petals
wild onion shoots
pimpernel leaves

method

For the champagne bread

Boil the milk with the jam, water, sugar and champagne. Place the pieces of bread in a bowl and pour the boiling liquid over them. Leave to soak for 24 hours.

For the champagne veil

Cold mix all the ingredients and boil them. Spread over a very thin plastic plate. Once gelled, cut into slices to cover the champagne bread.
Keep them on parchment paper until needed.

For the sugar crust

Mix the sugar with the egg and knead. Spread over a plate and place in the oven on parchment paper; sprinkle over the different powders. Bake at 50°C until it is completely dry and crisp.

For the champagne

Mix all of the ingredients and blend them. Leave to stand.

Arrange the champagne bread on a
plate covered with the crunchy veil.
Drizzle over the champagne. Cover all
the ingredients with the sugar crust.
Decorate around the 'ravioli' with
petals, leaves and orange zest etc.

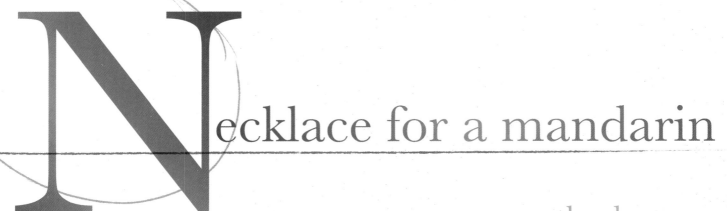

Necklace for a mandarin

ingredients

4 people

For the necklaces

350 g corn water (from a tin of sweetcorn)
100 g grape seed oil
40 g cornflour (cornstarch)
2 g salt
20 g fried corn powder

For the candied mandarin

2 mandarins
3 litres water
200 g sugar
100 g Cointreau

For the coconut and safflower ice cream

500 g milk
30 g dried coconut
200 g liquid cream
200 g sugar
300 g coconut milk
2 g safflower

For the mandarin gel

200 g preserved mandarins
40 g sugar
0.5 g xanthan gum

method

For the necklaces

Cold mix the ingredients except the corn powder.
Place a 15 cm diameter stainless steel ring in the centre of a 30 cm diameter non-stick pan (so that the space between the edges remains empty). Put 40 grams of the mixture in there to brown over a low heat. Remove the ring and then the necklace, with extreme care. Leave it to cool. Sprinkle with the corn powder. Set aside.

For the candied mandarin

Cook the mandarins in water for 5 minutes. Discard the water and repeat this operation three times. Finally, add the water (approx. 400 g), the sugar and alcohol, and simmer over low heat for 45 minutes. Leave to rest in the syrup. Then cut each mandarin in half.

For the coconut and safflower ice cream

Boil all the ingredients. Strain the mixture and place in the ice-cream maker until it is ready. Set aside.

For the mandarin gel

Drain the mandarins and mix with the other ingredients. Crush and strain. Set aside.

Fill the mandarins with the coconut ice cream and cover with a little gel. Place the maize necklace very carefully to one side.

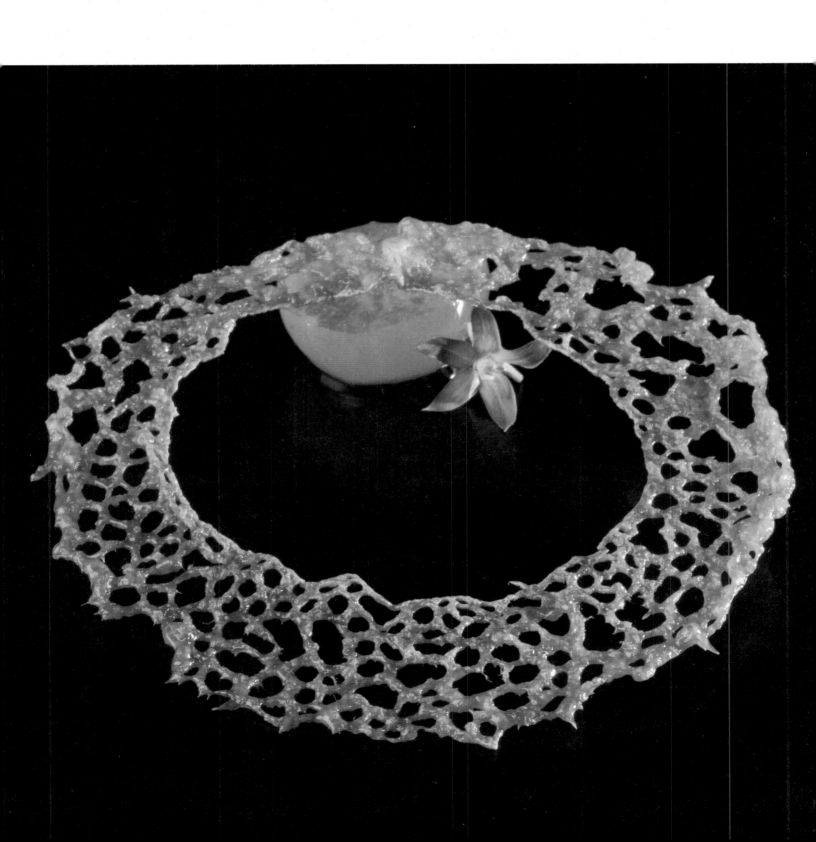

Chocolate and olive ice cream

ingredients

4 people

800 g milk
200 g cream
120 g sugar
100 g chocolate with 52% cocoa
1 g xanthan
200 g pitted black olives

method

Boil the milk with the cream and sugar.
Chop the chocolate and pour the boiling
milk over it. Stir well until the chocolate
melts completely into the milk.
Crush the olives with their juice and the
xanthan. Add the olive mixture to the
chocolate and blend to an homogeneous
mixture.

Place in an ice-cream maker and
serve at a suitable temperature
(between -3 and -5°C).

Passionate sponge cake

ingredients   method

4 people

For the cake

80 g butter
100 g passion fruit juice
30 g muscovado sugar
50 g flour
50 g almond flour
1 sachet of baking powder
120 g sugar
3 egg whites (beaten to snow)

For the crispy milk

400 g whole milk
4 g xanthan gum
8 g lyophilized (powdered) milk

For the orange and butter broth

100 g orange juice
30 g lemon juice
50 g water
30 g butter
35 g sugar

For the passionate cream

75 g passion fruit pulp
115 g sugar
2 egg whites

For the cake

Melt together the butter, passion fruit juice and muscovado sugar. Cool.
Add the flours, baking powder and sugar to this cold mixture. Mix well so that there are no lumps and incorporate the snowy egg whites.
Insert into a 1.5 litre rectangle cake mould and bake at 180°C for 8 minutes. Set aside.

For the crispy milk

Whisk the milk and the xanthan gum for 5 minutes. Spread out on paper and dry in the oven for 24 hours at 55°C. When it has dried, cut the dough into rectangles. Sprinkle with the powdered milk.

For the orange and butter broth

Boil all the ingredients and leave to cool. When cold, strain.

For the passionate cream

Beat the egg whites with 40 g sugar. In a saucepan, make a syrup with 75 g sugar and the fruit pulp, heat up to 121°C. When ready, add in the form of a thread to the egg whites, while beating them. Whisk together until the temperature reaches 30°C.
Leave to cool in the refrigerator.

Cut the cake into portions and soak for one minute in the orange and butter broth.
Arrange the soaked cake and place the crispy milk with the passionate cream beside it. Drizzle the broth at the bottom of the dish.

Soft drink precursor

Back in my youth, when soft drinks with cola stormed our country, their taste immediately became associated with the popular refreshing, non-alcoholic, soft drinks, which were then competing with juices and lemonades and even almond milk, especially in summer. They included a refreshing precursor to today's ubiquitous colas, sarsaparilla. But the truth is that at that time we knew hardly anything about it, apart from its peculiar pungent taste and freshness.

Sarsaparilla is a native South American plant that is distributed all over the world. It lives in the rainforests of the Americas from Mexico to Brazil. It can be seen in forests and thickets, covering tree trunks and shrubs.

It is a climbing, woody plant, with winding stems, bearing stingers. The leaves are shiny, leathery, sometimes with spiny margins and with two tendrils at the base. They can vary from heart-shaped to narrow and pointed, green in colour sometimes mottled with a paler green. The flowers are small, pale yellow, soft perfumed pendant inflorescences. There are male plants and female plants. The female has berries that mature from green to red and black. Most important are their long roots, as these are the parts of the plant that are used.

It is said that sarsaparilla is a great blood purifier and helps with rheumatism, skin problems, and even, apparently, sexual impotence and general weakness. It is also used as a health stimulant.

So far its culinary use has been somewhat limited. It is used in the preparation of soft drinks and as an industrial thickener for beer.

It is interesting to cite a veteran home-made drink called 'old-fashioned root beer', made with honey and hot water (as syrup), adding sarsaparilla extract and sparkling water, to give the necessary effervescence.

The culinary application we have just developed is based on a discovery we made some time ago. Surprisingly, with squid and crispy black pudding, far from dampening their flavours, it significantly enhances them.

Sealed baby squid

method

ingredients

For the baby squid

12 squid
salt
sarsaparilla powder
ginger

For the squid dressing

2 g chopped orange peel
2 g chopped lemon peel
1 g grated coconut
0.5 g dried garlic powder
0.5 g paprika
chopped parsley
25 g virgin olive oil
salt
sarsaparilla powder
ginger

For the sauce filling

250 g black squid ink
1 g xanthan gum
10 g fried bread cubes
½ peach, diced and sautéed with lemon
   verbena
pinch of powdered rooibos tea
pinch of dried ham powder
salt
ginger

For solid yellow sauce

1 onion
2 peaches
150 g mango pulp
3 tablespoons oil
1 g rooibos tea
8 g gellan gum (for 300 g sauce)
salt
white pepper

For the solid black sauce

1 sepia (300 g)
1 onion
2 green peppers
1 garlic clove
1 small tomato
25 ml olive oil
½ glass red wine
2.5 litres water
10 g gellan gum (for 300 g sauce)
salt

For the freeze-dried black sauce

100 g sepia ink

For the green oil

1 bunch fresh spring onions
250 ml grapeseed oil (alternatively,
   sunflower oil)
1 soup spoon sherry vinegar
salt

Present the baby squid, having
cooked them a la plancha with
a drop of oil, keeping the shape
indicated in the preparation.
Remove the paperclips. The
interior of the squid will hold the
liquid filling. Grate the black and
yellow sauces around the squid.
Dot with the green oil.

For the baby squid

Thoroughly clean the squid and separate
the bodies from the tentacles, fins etc. Save
the ink, tentacles and fins to make the sauce
for the filling.
Turn the squid inside out. Season them
and add the ginger and sarsaparilla. Lightly
brown the inside of the squid in a hot
pan. Turn them over again to regain their
original shape.

For the squid dressing

Mix all the ingredients. Keep the squid
in this mixture before cooking them a la
plancha.

For the sauce filling

Mix the ink with xanthan gum and add the
remaining ingredients; finally, add the tea,
ham and seasoning. Allow to cool.
Stuff the squid and close with metal clips
(paperclips).

For the solid yellow sauce

Cut the onion into julienne and sauté gently
in oil. When sweated, add the peaches and
sauté. Add the pulp, tea and gellan gum. Boil
well, blend and season.

For the solid black sauce

Chop the onion, peppers and garlic into fine
julienne; sauté in oil.
Clean the sepia and remove the ink. Chop
the sepia into not very small pieces.
Add to the sautéed vegetables and continue
to sauté everything. Incorporate the
chopped tomato and continue cooking until
it is almost gone. Moisten with wine and
reduce. Add the ink, diluted in water. Mix
everything together and cover with water.
Simmer about 30 minutes over medium
heat. Remove all the meat, blend the rest,
strain and add salt to taste.
Reserve some of the sauce for freeze-
drying. Boil the rest with the gellan gum.
Blend and season, if necessary.

For the freeze-dried black sauce

Place the ink in the freeze-drier; it will take
about 40 hours to dry.

For the green oil

Cut the spring onions into sticks and
marinate for a whole day in the grapeseed
oil, vinegar and salt. Then crush everything
and strain through a fine chinois.

Black pudding crunches

ingredients

4 people

For the frying batter

100 g water
90 g trisol
65 g flour
2 g dried yeast
10 g black sesame powder
1 g salt

For the morcilla ball

(interior)
360 g morcilla
150 g milk
1.5 g calcium

(exterior)
2 litres water
10 g alginate

In addition

pinch of sarsaparilla
oil for frying
flour

Scoop small spoonfuls of the morcilla mixture into the alginate bath. Leave for 5 minutes until the outer layer forms. There will be small spheres about the size of a small nut. Remove and sprinkle lightly with flour. Then dip in the frying batter and fry them in abundant hot oil.
Serve immediately sprinkled with sarsaparilla.

method

For the frying batter

Mix all the ingredients and leave to stand for an hour in the cold. Set aside.

For the morcilla ball

For the interior, roast the sausage at 180°C for half an hour. Crush with the other ingredients and strain. Set aside.
For the exterior, cold mix all the ingredients. Set aside until the next day.

General Index